New Efficiency Theory

Springer
*Berlin
Heidelberg
New York
Hong Kong
London
Milan
Paris
Tokyo*

Jati K. Sengupta

New Efficiency Theory

With Applications of Data Envelopment Analysis

With 23 Figures

Springer

Professor Dr. Jati K. Sengupta
University of California
Department of Economics
Santa Barbara, CA 93106
USA
sengupta@econ.ucsb.edu

ISBN 3-540-14013-1 Springer-Verlag Berlin Heidelberg New York

Cataloging-in-Publication Data applied for
A catalog record for this book is available from the Library of Congress.
Bibliographic information published by Die Deutsche Bibliothek
Die Deutsche Bibliothek lists this publication in the Deutsche Nationalbibliografie; detailed bibliographic data is available in the Internet at <http://dnb.ddb.de>.

This work is subject to copyright. All rights are reserved, whether the whole or part of the material is concerned, specifically the rights of translation, reprinting, reuse of illustrations, recitation, broadcasting, reproduction on microfilm or in any other way, and storage in data banks. Duplication of this publication or parts thereof is permitted only under the provisions of the German Copyright Law of September 9, 1965, in its current version, and permission for use must always be obtained from Springer-Verlag. Violations are liable for prosecution under the German Copyright Law.

Springer-Verlag Berlin Heidelberg New York
a member of BertelsmannSpringer Science+Business Media GmbH

http://www.springer.de

© Springer-Verlag Berlin · Heidelberg 2003
Printed in Germany

The use of general descriptive names, registered names, trademarks, etc. in this publication does not imply, even in the absence of a specific statement, that such names are exempt from the relevant protective laws and regulations and therefore free for general use.

Hardcover-Design: Erich Kirchner, Heidelberg

SPIN 10928493   42/3130-5 4 3 2 1 0 – Printed on acid-free paper

To: **Thakur and Holy Mother**

Preface

New efficiency theory refers to the various parametric and semi-parametric methods of estimating production and cost frontiers, which include data envelopment analysis (DEA) with its diverse applications in management science and operations research. This monograph develops and generalizes the new efficiency theory by highlighting the interface between economic theory and operations research.

Some of the outstanding features of this monograph are: (1) integrating the theory of firm efficiency and industry equilibrium, (2) emphasizing growth efficiency in a dynamic setting, (3) incorporating uncertainty of market demand and prices, and (4) the implications of group efficiency by sharing investments. New applications discuss in some detail the growth and decline of US computer industry, the relative performance of mutual fund portfolios and the implications of applying a game-theoretic view of efficiency, when firms can form coalitions of different sizes.

The central focus of this monograph is on applications of DEA models and their dynamic and stochastic implications. The volume includes a large part of my research work on efficiency theory over the last five years. My sincere appreciation to all my research students, who have helped me develop and empirically apply the new efficiency theory. Finally, I owe a deep appreciation to my wife, who has constantly provided me support and encouragement. Her silent support in the background meant so much for my research work.

Jati K. Sengupta

Contents

Preface vii

1. **New Approaches to Economic Efficiency** 1
   1.1 New Theory 2
   1.2 New Applications 10

2. **Sources of Economic Efficiency** 15
   2.1 Learning by Doing 16
   2.2 Technology and Productivity Growth 32

3. **Cost Oriented Efficiency** 52
   3.1 Data Envelopment Analysis 52
   3.2 Industry Equilibrium 56

4. **Competition and Efficiency** 70
   4.1 Growth Frontier 73
   4.2 Efficiency in Industry Equilibrium 82

5. **Growth and Efficiency in Computer Industry** 101
   5.1 Sales Growth and Decline 107
   5.2 Technical Change and Scale Efficiency 112

6. **Efficiency Under Uncertainty** 117
   6.1 Cost and Demand Uncertainty 117
   6.2 Efficiency in Capital Markets 130

7. **Input Sharing and Efficiency** 146
   7.1 Efficiency in the Core 146
   7.2 Shared Investment and Group Efficiency 151

8. **Modeling and Data Problems** 160
   8.1 Modeling Issues 160
   8.2 DEA Models Under Nonstationarity 161

Index 175

1
New Approaches to Economic Efficiency

Measuring productive efficiency of firms or enterprises and analyzing their policy implications have been a central topic of research in microeconomic theory. Recently some new approaches have been proposed, since the method of data envelopment analysis (DEA) was first proposed by Charnes, Cooper and Rhodes (1978). These new approaches develop a nonparametric class of measurement of relative efficiency of firms within an industry, which uses observed input output data to characterize a production frontier. The concept of technical efficiency underlies the production frontier i.e., an input output vector is said to be technically efficient, if and only if increasing any output or decreasing any input is possible only by decreasing some other output or increasing some other input. Fare, Grosskopf and Lovell (1994) have surveyed this field of production frontiers and discussed the contributions of Koopmans, Debreu, Farrell and others.

New extensions of the nonparametric class of efficiency measurement have taken several forms of which the following are the most significant:

(a) Cost oriented DEA models, where the influence of market demand affects the cost output relations of firms and their entry and exit behavior in the industry;

(b) The interdependence of firms and its effect on industry equilibrium framework for the DEA class of nonparametric models;

(c) The informational basis of input output and cost data explores the impact of asymmetry and heterogeneity on the efficiency measures such as technical and allocative efficiency;

(d) The role of uncertainty and risk in the production process and the overall market demand has important impact on both technical and allocative efficiency. Whereas technical or production efficiency measures the firm's success in producing maximum output from a given set of inputs, the allocative or price efficiency measures the firm's success in choosing an optimal set of inputs with a given set of input prices determined by the overall market. Fluctuations in demand and market prices of inputs and outputs have significant impact on the optimal choice of inputs and outputs by firms.

Our objectives in this chapter are two-fold. One is to present a broad overview of the four aspects of new efficiency theory outlined above and to discuss some empirical applications in specific industries such as computers and stock market portfolios. Whereas the computer industry is highly technology-intensive, the portfolio investment field illustrates the complex problem of characterizing efficiency under conditions of market fluctuations, which affect the probability distribution of returns, their means and variances. Heterogeneity of data and nonstationarity of inputs and outputs provide additional reasons for characterizing efficiency measures, which are relatively stable in some statistical sense.

1.1 New Theory

A cost oriented efficiency model provides a more general framework than a production efficiency approach for several reasons. First, a cost function is well defined even in cases of increasing returns to scale and a firm or DMU (decision making unit) can minimize overall costs for any given level of output. Thus a cost frontier can be derived from the cost-minimizing model

$$\text{Min TC} = \sum_{i=1}^{m} q_i x_i$$

subject to (s.t.) $y \leq f(x_1, x_2, \ldots, x_m)$

where q_i are input prices or unit costs and $f(\cdot)$ denotes the production function. If the production function is of a Cobb-Douglas form $f(x_1, x_2) = A x_1^{b_1} x_2^{b_2}$, the cost minimization yields the cost frontier

$$\ln c^* = k_o + \sum_{i=1}^{2} k_i \ln q_i + a \ln y^*$$

where $k_i = b_i / \sum_{i=1}^{2} b_i$, $a = (b_1 + b_2)^{-1}$ and k_o is a suitable constant depending on b_1, b_2 and A. Clearly any observed cost c_j for firm j can be written as

$$\ln c_j = \ln c_j^* + v_j; \quad v_j \geq 0$$

In order to test the relative cost efficiency of a firm h, a DEA model can then be set up as follows:

$$\text{Min } v_h = \ln c_h - \ln c_h^*$$
$$\text{s.t. } \ln c_j^* \leq \ln c_j; \quad j=1,2,...,N$$

If firm h is cost efficient, then $\ln c_h = \ln c_h^*$; otherwise it is relatively inefficient.

For a linear cost frontier a DEA model can be set up as a linear programming (LP) model:

$$\text{Min } \theta$$
$$\text{s.t. } \sum_{j=1}^{N} c_j \lambda_j \leq \theta c_h; \sum_{j=1}^{N} y_j \lambda_j \geq y_h$$
$$\sum \lambda_j = 1; \lambda_j \geq 0; j=1,2,...,N$$

If at the optimal solution $\left(\lambda_j^*, \theta^*\right)$ it holds that $\theta^* = 1$ and all slack variables are zero, then the unit h is relatively cost efficient and by duality the cost frontier can be easily derived as

$$c_h^* = (\beta_0/\beta_1) + (\alpha/\beta_1) y_h = b_0 + b_1 y_h$$

where β_1, α and β_0 are the appropriate Lagrange multipliers for the LP problem above.

Clearly other nonlinear forms of the cost frontier can be formulated in terms of the DEA model. Thus if the cost frontier is quadratic and strictly convex, the LP model would be of the form

$$\text{Min } v_h = c_h - c_h^*$$
$$\text{s.t. } c_j^* \leq c_j; \quad j=1,2,...,N$$

where $c_j^* = b_0 + b_1 y_j + b_2 y_j^2$. The dual of this model can be written as

$$\text{Min } \theta$$
$$\text{s.t. } \sum_j c_j \lambda_j \leq \theta c_h; \sum y_j \lambda_j \geq y_h; \sum y_j^2 \lambda_j \geq y_h^2 \quad (1)$$
$$\sum \lambda_j = 1, \lambda_j \geq 0; j = 1, 2, ..., N$$

Let $\left(\lambda_j^*, \theta^*\right)$ be the optimal solution with all slack variables zero. Then if $\theta^* = 1$, firm h is on the cost frontier, i.e., $c_h = c_h^*$. But if $0 < \theta^* < 1$, then there exists a convex combination of other firms such that $\sum \lambda_j^* c_j < c_h$, i.e. firm or unit h is not on the cost efficiency frontier. This convex hull method of determining cost efficiency through the LP model uses only the observed data on total costs and output for each firm.

Cost Efficiency Models

The cost efficiency models above can be generalized in several directions. The adjustment cost approach, which views both static and dynamic components of the production function is an obvious generalization. The adjustment cost is usually introduced in a firm's decision problem to explain why it finds it optimal to spread the planned adjustments in inputs and output to long run equilibrium over time. Sengupta (1999) has shown how adjustment costs can be incorporated in the DEA framework.

As a second generalization consider the quadratic cost frontier derived from the LP model (1) as

$$c_j = b_0 + b_1 y_j + b_2 y_j^2$$

The average cost is

$$AC_j = (b_0 / y_j) + b_1 + b_2 y_j$$

On minimizing this average cost one obtains

$$y_j^* = (b_0 / b_2)^{1/2}; AC(y_j^*) = b_1 + 2\sqrt{b_0 b_2}$$

This output level y_j^* may be called the optimal capacity output, since it specifies the most optimal level of capacity utilization. Since marginal cost is $MC_j = b_1 + 2b_2 y_j^*$ we have $MC_j = AC_j$ at the optimal capacity output y_j^* for the efficient firm j. Under competition the firm is a price taker, hence the market price p equals MC_j. Under free entry, if $p > MC_j$ new firms enter the market till the equilibrium prevails with an optimal number of firms in the industry. The dynamics of the entry and exit behavior and the impact of relative economic efficiency of firms in an industry open up a new frontier of DEA research. This is discussed in some detail in later chapters of this book.

Asymmetric Information

The DEA models usually assume that the input output and cost data are all observed and available to all DMUs. Also, the DMUs are assumed to exhibit their best performance under the given environment. However in reality this may not be true. The information structure (IS) underlying the observed data may be of different forms, of which the following are most significant. First of all, the data may contain random or unsystematic noise elements. The DMUs may react to the underlying randomness by adopting a risk averse behavior. Also, the probability distribution of the random components may not be completely known to different DMUs. Secondly, when we deal with allocative efficiency models in DEA framework, market prices of inputs and output may contain random components and the DMUs may use expected prices to determine the optimal inputs and output. Thirdly, the IS may evolve over time so that the DMUs learn from the past trend and they may form rational expectations of future prices in order to compute the optimal mix of inputs.

Another important class of IS is posed by asymmetric information. Here we consider the DEA model as a principal-agent problem between a DMU as an agent and its owner or regulator the principal. Here it is assumed that the agent has specific information about the costs of different outputs, while the principal only knows the output levels and their associated costs in a given environment. The asymmetry in IS allows the agents to extract more information rents from the principal when a new production plan is introduced. This type of cost-oriented model has been discussed in some detail by Dalen (1993), Wunsch (1994) and Bogetoft (2000). Thus, Dalen considers a model with two DMUs, one input (x_i) and one output (y_i)

$$x_i = (\beta + s_i) y_i$$

where x_i is cost for DMU_i and β a cost parameter known only to the DMUs and s_i is the slack chosen by DMU_i. Dalen discusses the effect of using the best announced unit cost $min\{\beta + s_1, \beta + s_2\}$ as opposed to the individually announced costs $\beta + s_1$ and $\beta + s_2$ when allocating a fixed budget among the DMUs. He showed that the competition for limited funds might be reduced when best announced costs are used. Wunsch considers a similar framework to compare the use of individual versus best practice reimbursement schemes in a single input (x_i), single output (y_i) cost model

$$x_i = c(y_i) + s_i$$

where $c(\cdot)$ is an increasing function known only to the DMUs but not the regulator. The regulator only observes (x_i, y_i) expost. Wunsch shows that best practice standards of the so-called free disposal hull type may reduce the informational rents.

Bogetoft considers the problem of deciding which optimal production plans to choose in the future, given the asymmetric IS of the principal-agent framework. He considers several types of communication setting between the principal and the agent e.g., (1) standard setting with no communication where actual costs are not verifiable, (2) verifiable setting, where actual costs are verifiable expost and therefore can be contracted upon and (3) decentralized setting, where the principal can inform the agent about the set of acceptable production plans and check expost whether or not the agent did actually implement a plan from the set of acceptable plans.

The decentralization aspect of this type of formulation is most interesting for a competitive industry framework. In order to illustrate his analysis we consider his model where the principal delegates the production of m products to an agent, whose minimal cost of producing outputs y is assumed to be linear $c(y) = c'y$. It is assumed that the agent's actual cost (x) in the planning period is

$$x = c(y) + s$$

where the scalar slack variable s is extra cost. The agent knows $c(\cdot)$ but the principal does not. The principal however knows from previous periods the costs and outputs of n feasible production plans (x^i, y^i) for the n agents i = 1,2,...,n. Hence he can infer with certainty that

$$c \in C = \left\{ c \in R^m \mid c'y^i \leq x^i; i = 1, 2, ..., n \right\}$$

where prime denotes the transpose of a vector. The principal's belief about the likelihood of different cost functions may be assumed to be given by a probability distribution $p(\cdot)$ on C. This belief distribution is used to close the model as a Bayesian game.

The two optimization models, one for the principal and the other for the agent may then be set up. The principal's overall problem may be set up as one of maximizing the benefits minus costs,

$$\max_y B(y) - c_T(y) \qquad (2)$$

where $B(y)$ is the benefits and $c_T(y)$ is total costs, including production and incentive costs. The agent in this framework seeks to maximize his utility U_A, which is a weighted combination of his profit and slack

$$\max U_A = (b-x) + \rho(x - c'y), \quad 0 < \rho < 1 \qquad (3)$$

where y is the implemented production plan, b is the monetary transfer from the principal to the agent and x is the actual costs.

Note that the different communication settings can be formulated as special cases and restrictions of the above models defined by (2) and (3). Thus the 'second best solutions' can be defined when restrictions on full communication of information are imposed. Finally, the decentralization algorithms of competitive equilibrium can be easily introduced in this framework, where the overall market acts as the principal and the agents are the individual firms competing for the least cost solution.

Efficiency Under Uncertainty

Two types of uncertainty have generally been considered in the DEA literature. One is the case of uncertainty in future demand, which may result in either incomplete knowledge of the input and output prices, or inventories and shortages when supply does not match demand. In case of incomplete price information the firms or decision making units (DMUs) may consider the riskiness of alternative production plans due to price fluctuations and allow for these in terms of the means and variances of prices and then define an optimal risk adjusted production plan with a given degree of risk aversion. Sengupta (1999, 2000) has discussed this type of *risk averse efficiency frontier* approach in both static and dynamic forms in the DEA framework.

Secondly, the incompleteness of information about the inputs and outputs available to different DMUs raises the important policy problem: whether a coordination or pooling of information structures may improve the overall efficiency? This question is most critical in deciding on the optimal allocation of research knowledge and investments for R&D, where learning by doing phenomena may exist. Unlike Bogetoft (2000) who discusses the impact on efficiency from the asymmetric information structures, we discuss here the consequences of information pooling or forming a club with aggregated resources. So long as this process of pooling increases efficiency through *economies of scope*, when compared with the individualistic production without any information sharing or pooling, we have the problem of deciding on the optimal mix or the optimal degree of pooling.

Another type of risk analysis arises in the optimal investment problem in the capital market when the asset prices are fluctuating over time. Here the parametric approach of the mean variance theory of portfolio investments and its various extensions may be recast in a nonparametric way in terms of a DEA approach. For example the relative performance of different mutual fund portfolios may be compared and also utilized to construct an efficiency frontier. Since riskiness measured by variance of returns may be viewed as costs along with other costs such as loads and other transaction costs, the mean variance efficiency analysis can be easily generalized so as to include skewness of return and correlations with the overall market represented by such an index as S&P 500. This aspect will be discussed in some detail in Chapter 6.

The impact of fluctuations of demand and prices on efficiency may be analyzed in terms of allocative efficiency and overall efficiency. To characterize overall efficiency (OE_h) of a DMU_h or firm h, one may set up the following DEA model for determining the optimal input vector x with given input prices $w = (w_1,\ldots,w_m)$:

$$\text{Min } c = w'x$$
$$\text{s.t. } \sum_{j}^{N} x(j)\lambda_j \leq x; \sum_{j=1}^{N} y(j)\lambda_j \geq y_h \qquad (4)$$
$$\sum_{j=1}^{N} \lambda_j = 1; \lambda_j \geq 0; j = 1, 2, \ldots, N$$

Here w is an m-element vector of input costs or prices as determined in the competitive market, x(j) and y(j) are input output vectors with m and n elements respectively for each DMUj and x is the input vector to be optimally decided by the DMU_h or firm h. This is an input-oriented model for determining overall efficiency. If output prices p are given, then the objective function (4) may be rewritten as a profit function i.e.,

$$\text{Max } \pi = p'y - w'x$$

and the vector y_h in the second constraint replaced by the output vector y to be determined along with the input vector x. Let $\lambda = (\lambda_j^*)$ and x^* be the optimal solutions of the DEA model (4) with all slack variables zero in the optimal basis. Then the minimal cost is given by $c^* = w'x(h) = c_h^*$. The overall efficiency (OE_h) of DMU_h is then measured by

$$OE_h = c_h^* / c_h = TE_h \cdot AE_h \tag{5}$$

Here TE_h is technical efficiency measured by θ^* in the optimal solution of the input oriented DEA model

$$\begin{aligned} &\text{Min } \theta \\ &\text{s.t.} \sum_{j=1}^{N} x(j)\lambda_j \leq \theta x(h); \sum_{j=1}^{N} y(j)\lambda_j \geq y(h) \\ &\sum \lambda_j = 1, \lambda_j \geq 0; j \in I_N = \{1, 2, ..., N\} \end{aligned} \tag{6}$$

Hence allocative efficiency (AE_h) of DMU_h is measured by $AE_h = c_h^* / (\theta^* c_h)$. Clearly if $\theta^* x(h) = x^*$, then DMU_h is both technically and allocatively efficient, i.e., $TE_h = 1.0 = AE_h$ and hence $OE_h = 1.0$.

The decomposition (5) of overall economic efficiency has two important economic implications. One is that the technical (production) efficiency is a necessary but not sufficient condition for overall economic efficiency. Secondly, if DMU_h reaches the market equilibrium in the sense that at $x(h) = x^*$ the iso-quant is tangent to the price line, then both TE_h and AE_h attain the value unity indicating both technical and allocative efficiency. But in case of disequilibrium, i.e., at a nontangency point the two efficiencies may diverge and sometimes significantly. For instance Sueyoshi (1997) estimated by DEA models the three measures TE, AE and OE for the NTT telephone industry in Japan over the 39 year period 1953-92 and the equilibrium condition defined by the tangency of the iso-quant and the price line was satisfied by only 17.9% of the points, which implies that disequilibrium conditions prevailed for 82.1% of the DMUs. This shows the predominance of the disequilibrium points. One primary reason for this situation is due to the uncertainty associated with the vector w of prices. When the prices are known with certainty, the optimal input vector x* can be determined with certainty. But when only the probability distribution of w is known, only the distribution of optimal costs c* = w'x* can be determined e.g., the cumulative distribution F(c*) can be computed once the distribution F(w) of w is given or estimated. If G(c) denotes the cumulative distribution of observed cost c = w'x, then the statistical distance between the two distributions F(c*) and G(c) e.g., Kolmogorov-Smirnov distance may be used to characterize the distribution of relative inefficiencies.

When there are only few samples and the distribution F(w) of w cannot be estimated, we have a case of uncertainty. In such cases one may formulate a class of minimax decision rules for choosing optimal x. Thus let W denote the domain of vector w and X denote the constraint set given by (4). For each $x \in X$ we consider the worst-case scenario of costs by $\max_{w \in W} w'x$ and then minimize with respect to $x \in X$ i.e.,

$$\min_{x \in X} \left\{ \max_{w \in W} w'x \mid x \in X, w \in W \right\} \qquad (7)$$

In a more general case let $\hat{c}(w, x)$ denote the weighted combination of worst and best cost scenarios i.e., $\hat{c}(w, x) = \alpha \max_{w \in W} w'x + (1-\alpha) \min_{w \in W} w'x$ with $0 \leq \alpha \leq 1$ then a general class of decision rules may be formulated as

$$\min_{x \in X} \left\{ \hat{c}(w, x) \mid x \in X, w \in W \right\} \qquad (8)$$

Recently Kuosmanen and Post (2001) considered these types of measures as upper and lower bounds for cost efficiency. This type of analysis introduces a new type of stochastic analysis of DEA models of efficiency and it introduces a new frontier in applied efficiency research.

1.2 New Applications

Developments in new efficiency theory based on the nonparametric DEA approach have followed three important phases. The first phase used the engineering concept of efficiency as a ratio of weighted outputs to weighted inputs. This is the concept of technical or production efficiency where the prices are not used at all. Hence this measure of efficiency was widely applied in public sector enterprises, where output prices are either unavailable or determined outside the private markets. Typical applications here included public schools and colleges, county clinics and hospitals and government enterprises such as postal service and municipal activities. The second phase considered applications in the private sector such as commercial banking, airlines and transportation industries, where market prices determined by competitive markets played an active role. In this phase the allocative or price efficiency concept was used along with technical efficiency. This phase emphasized more on the cost frontier than the production frontier and hence price cost data proved to be equally important as the physical input output data.

The third phase considered various types of dynamic and stochastic aspects associated with technical and allocative efficiency. Dynamic aspects involve time series data on inputs, outputs and prices, which may involve a short or a long run production horizon. Some inputs e.g., capital may be fixed in the short run, although they may vary in the long run. Hence output growth over time may be due to input growth and price changes over time. In this growth perspective one may distinguish between level efficiency and growth efficiency. The former relates output levels to inputs, whereas the latter explains output growth by input growth. Thus the former yields technical level efficiency, whereas the latter technical growth efficiency.

In this book we discuss mostly the empirical applications in the third phase. The computer industry is studied in some detail, since it exhibits many dynamic characteristics of technological innovation and intensive market competition. Historically over the last two decades this industry has experienced substantial technological progress and efficiency growth. Some firms could not remain on the leading edge of the efficiency frontier over time, hence had to exit. Other firms on the efficiency frontier increased their market share and prospered. Changes in prices have also been substantial for this industry.

Applications of technical efficiency analysis of information technology (IT) investments are most important in modern technology-intensive industries such as microelectronics, semiconductor, telecommunications and computer industry. Recently Shao and Lin (2002) applied DEA models to 370 firms over 1988-1992 from Computerworld Surveys of Fortune 500 firms in order to examine the effects of IT on productivity, scale and profitability.

Another type of new application involves market fluctuations. Market volatility has been most prominent in the stock market over the last three years and returns on investment portfolios such as mutual funds have exhibited wide fluctuations. The so-called capital market model (CAPM) of market efficiency based primarily on the mean variance theory of portfolio choice has been frequently viewed as inadequate and imperfect. The application of the nonparametric DEA approach and its semi-parametric extensions in this framework provides new insight into the risky decision making process under markets exhibiting fluctuations in prices and returns.

Finally, the game theory application of the DEA efficiency model offers a new area of research, which has a significant potential for application in new areas. The principal and agent framework introduced by Dalen (1993) and Bogetoft (2000) has been already mentioned. A market game where the firms compete and the industry selects the most efficient firms provides another example. The Walrasian *tatonnement* process may then represent the different rounds of the play, which may or may not converge to equilibrium.

Consider for instance a special version of the DEA efficiency model, where each firm j produces a single output y_j with m inputs x_{ij}. In order to test the relative efficiency of firm k one sets up the LP model

$$\min_{\beta} g_k = \sum_{i=1}^{m} \beta_i x_{ik}$$
$$\text{s.t.} \quad \sum_{i=1}^{m} \beta_i x_{ij} \geq y_j; \quad j=1,2,\ldots,n \tag{9}$$
$$\beta_i \geq 0; \quad i=1,2,\ldots,n$$

The dual of this problem is

$$\max_{\lambda} z = \sum_{j=1}^{n} y_j \lambda_j$$
$$\text{s.t.} \quad \sum_{j=1}^{n} x_{ij} \lambda_j \leq x_{ik}; \quad i=1,2,\ldots,m \tag{10}$$
$$\lambda_j \geq 0; \quad j=1,2,\ldots,n$$

Now assume that the n firms form a set N = {1,2,…,n} of n players who can form coalitions (or mergers) of different sizes from two, three up to n. Let S be a coalition of less than n players and N the grand coalition of all n players. Then one may set up the following LP model as a generalization of the model (9):

$$\max_z = \sum_{j \in S} y_j \lambda_j$$
$$\text{s.t.} \quad \sum_{j \in S} x_{ij} \lambda_j \leq \hat{x}_i, \quad i = 1, 2, \ldots, m \tag{11}$$

where $\hat{x}_i = \hat{x}_i(S)$ is a particular allocation of input i from the total amount $\sum_{j \in S} x_{ij}$ of input i that the coalition has. We may thus define a characteristic function v(S) for the coalition S, which is a subset of the grand coalition N in terms of the model (11): $v(S) = \max \sum_{j \in S} y_j \lambda_j$. Since the inputs and outputs are all positive, it is easy to show that this input allocation game has a non-empty core and hence a non-empty set of allocations. Thus in practical applications one could analyze the various optimal solutions resulting from coalitions of different sizes. Thus, let S_1 and S_2 be two mutually disjoint coalitions of the grand coalition N, then so long as $v(S_1) > v(S_2) > 0$, one can improve the total payoff and hence overall efficiency by a reallocation process.

Several incentives exist in practical situations of a market game, when firms may form coalitions or mergers. One incentive is that a firm can reduce its costs $g_k = \beta' x_k$ by agreeing to cooperate in a coalition S. Thus the minimal cost $g_k = \beta' x_k$ defined in (9) can be lowered for some $k \in S$. A second advantage is that the input allocation game defined in (11) can be used to characterize a non-empty core and hence a non-empty set of allocations. This aspect of efficiency in the core would be discussed in some detail in Chapter 7.

Thus we conclude that the new approaches to economic efficiency emphasize both nonparametric and semi-parametric formulations of relative efficiency and illustrate these in terms of modern technology-intensive industries, where technological change and market fluctuations are most predominant.

References

- Bogetoft, P. (2000): DEA and Activity Planning Under Asymmetric Information. Journal of Productivity Analysis 13, 7-48
- Charnes, A., Cooper, W.W. and Rhodes, E. (1978): Measuring the Efficiency of Decision Making Units. European Journal of Operational Research 2, 429-444
- Dalen, D.M. (1993); Strategic Responses to Relative Evaluations of Bureaus: Implications for Bureaucratic Slack. Working paper, Department of Economics, University of Oslo, Norway
- Fare, R., Grosskopf, S., Knox Lovell, C.A. (1994): Production Frontiers, Cambridge University Press, New York
- Kuosmanen, T., Post, T. (2001): Measuring Economic Efficiency with Incomplete Price Information: With an Application to European Commercial Banks. European Journal of Operational Research 134, 43-58
- Sengupta, J.K. (1999): The Measurement of Dynamic Productive Efficiency. Bulletin of Economic Research 51, 111-124
- Sengupta, J.K. (2000): Dynamic and Stochastic Efficiency Analysis: Economics of Data Envelopment Analysis. World Scientific, London
- Shao, B., Lin, W., (2002): Technical Efficiency Analysis of Information Technology Investments: A Two-Stage Empirical Investigation. Information and Management 39, 391-401
- Sueyoshi, T. (1997): Measuring Efficiencies and Returns to Scale of Nippon Telegraph and Telephone in Production and Cost Analyses. Management Science 43, 779-796
- Wunsch, P. (1994): Peer Comparisons, Regulation and Replicability. Working Paper, CORE, Belgium

2
Sources of Economic Efficiency

In recent times competition has been most intense in the modern high-tech industries in Silicon Valley in US, such as semiconductors, microelectronics and personal computers. Product and process innovations, economies of scale and learning by doing have intensified the competitive pressure leading to declining prices and unit costs. Thus Norsworthy and Jang (1992) in their measurement of technological change in these industries over the last decade noted the high degree of cost efficiency due to learning by doing and R&D investment. More recently the empirical study by Jorgenson and Stiroh (2000) noted two significant impacts of the growth of computer power on the overall US economy. First, as the production of computers improves and becomes more efficient, more computing power is being produced from the same inputs, i.e., learning by doing. This increases the overall economic growth. Secondly, the computer using industries are now using skilled labor working with better computer equipment, thus increasing labor productivity in these industries. Thus the average industry productivity growth (i.e., total factor productivity growth in a specific industry) has achieved a rate of 2.0 percent per year over the period 1958-96 for electronic equipment, which include semiconductors and communications equipment. High productivity growth led to falling unit costs and prices. For instance, average computer prices declined by 18 percent per year from 1960 to 1995 and by 27.6 percent per year over 1995-98. R&D investments and learning by doing have contributed significantly to this trend of decline in unit costs and prices.

Our object in this chapter is threefold. One is to formulate a set of *nonparametric* and *semiparametric* models of production and cost frontier of a high-tech industry, where firms survive the intense competition if they maintain dynamic efficiency over time. Secondly, the impact of learning by doing on production and cost efficiency of firms is specifically introduced in this nonparametric and dynamic framework. Finally, we compare the level and growth efficiency of firms, where the former characterizes the output level along a production frontier, whereas the latter follows Solow (1997) in considering a state of sustained growth of output due to faster technological progress. R&D investments may contribute to this process of technological progress.

Most of the nonparametric models do not use any specific form of the production or cost function; they are based on the observed levels of inputs, output and their growth over time. Technological progress (regress) is measured in this framework by the proportional rate of growth (decline) of total factor productivity (TFP), where TFP is defined as the ratio of aggregate output to aggregate input.

The plan of the paper is as follows. Section 2.1 discusses the static framework of the nonparametric models of economic efficiency, where learning by doing is introduced in several forms. We have utilized here the convex hull method of characterizing the efficient points by a sequence of linear programming (LP) formulations pioneered initially by Farrell (1957) and later extended as DEA (data envelopment analysis) models in management science and operations research literature. Section 2.2 develops a cost frontier model in terms of level efficiency and growth efficiency and relates the analysis to a production frontier model. This is followed by an illustrative empirical application to the US computer industry over the period 1987-98.

2.1 Learning by Doing

Several types of learning by doing in the production process have been discussed in the current literature. For example, Jovanovic (1997) has recently classified learning models into two broad types: one associated with technology and the other with human capital. We would consider here only the human capital aspect, which affects both quality and productivity improvements. Three types of measures of learning are used in our formulation. One is the cumulative research experience embodied in cumulative output, where the latter is very often taken as a measure of technological progress, e.g., the empirical studies of industrial productivity by Norsworthy and Jang (1992) have found the cost reducing effect of such technological progress to be substantial in microelectronics, telecommunications and similar other industries. The second measure is cumulative experience embodied in the strategic inputs such as capital goods in Arrow's model. The R&D expenditures allocated to improve the quality of any or all inputs may be considered here. Finally, the experience in 'knowledge capital' available to a firm due to a spillover from other firms may be embodied in the cost function of the firm through cumulative research inputs.

The nonparametric efficiency analysis is specified here in terms of a series of linear programming (LP) models. The unifying theme of these models is a convex hull method of characterizing the production frontier (also called technical efficiency) without using any market prices and the cost frontier (also called allocative efficiency), which uses market prices to determine the optimal levels of inputs. While the production frontier model is used in LP models (1) and (21) in their static and dynamic versions, the cost frontier model is used in the LP models (3) and (24). The cost frontier model is more suitable in the dynamic framework, since R&D expenditure and learning experience can be directly related to the marginal costs, although the various components of R&D expenditure and learning are difficult to specify in terms of separate physical inputs.

Consider now a standard input oriented nonparametric model, also known as a DEA (data envelopment analysis) model for testing the relative efficiency of a reference firm or decision making unit h(DMU_h) in a cluster of N units, where each DMU_j produces s outputs (y_{rj}) with two types of inputs: m physical inputs (x_{ij}) and n R&D inputs as knowledge capital (z_{wj}):

$$\text{Min } \theta + \phi, \text{ subject to } \sum_{j=1}^{N} X_j \lambda_j \leq \theta X_h ; \sum_{j=1}^{N} Z_j \lambda_j \leq \phi Z_h \quad (1)$$

$$\sum_{j=1}^{N} Y_j \lambda_j \geq Y_h ; \sum_j \lambda_j \geq 0; \quad j = 1, 2, ..., N$$

Here X_j, Z_j and Y_j are the observed input and output vectors for each DMU_j, where j=1,2,...,N. Let $\lambda^* = (\lambda_j^*)$, θ^*, ϕ^* be the optimal solutions of model (1) with all slacks zero. Then the reference unit or firm h is said to be *technically efficient* if $\theta^* = 1.0 = \phi^*$. If however θ^* and ϕ^* are positive but less than unity, then it is not technically efficient at the 100% level, since it uses excess inputs measured by (1-θ^*) x_{ih} and (1-ϕ^*) z_{wh}. Overall efficiency (OE_j) of a unit j however combines the technical (TE_j) or production efficiency and the allocative (AE_j) or price efficiency as follows: $OE_j = TE_j \times AE_j$. To measure overall efficiency of a DMU_h one solves the cost minimizing model:

$$\text{Min } C = c'x + q'z$$
$$\text{s.t. } X\lambda \leq x; Z\lambda \leq z; Y\lambda \geq Y_h; \lambda'e = 1; \lambda \geq 0 \quad (2)$$

where e is a column vector with N elements each of which is unity, prime denotes transpose, c and q are unit cost vectors of the two types of inputs x and z which are now the decision variables and $X = (X_j)$, $Z = (Z_j)$ and $Y = (Y_j)$ are appropriate matrices of observed inputs and outputs. Denoting optimal values by asterisks, technical efficiency is $TE_h = \theta^* + \phi^*$ as before, overall efficiency (OE_h) is C_h^* / C_h computed from model (2) and hence the allocative efficiency is $AE_h = C_h^*/(\theta^*+\phi^*)C_h$, where C_h and C_h^* are the observed and optimal costs for unit h.

Now consider the special characteristics of the research inputs z. Since these inputs lower the initial unit production costs c_i and also affect the cost function nonlinearly we can rewrite the objective function of (2) as

$$\text{Min TC} = \sum_i \left[(c_i - f_i(\sum_w q_w z_w))x_i + \tfrac{1}{2} d_i x_i^2 \right] + \tfrac{1}{2} \sum_{w=1}^m g_w z_w^2 \qquad (3)$$

subject to the constraints of model (2). Here f_i is the unit cost reduction with $f_i < c_i$ and the component cost functions are assumed to be strictly convex implying diminishing returns to the underlying R&D production function. The optimal solutions z_w, x_i and λ_i now must satisfy the Kuhn-Tucker necessary conditions as follows:

$$f_i q_w x_i + \gamma_w \le g_w z_w; z_w \ge 0$$
$$f_i(\sum q_w z_w) + \beta_i \le c_i + d_i x_i \ge 0 \qquad (4)$$

If the unit (DMU_h) is efficient with positive input levels and zero slacks, then we must have equality $\partial L/\partial z_w = 0 = \partial L/\partial x_i$ where L is the Lagrangean function. Hence we can write the optimal values (z_w^*, x_i^*) as:

$$z_w^* = (f_i q_w x_i^* + \gamma_w^*)/g_w; w=1,2,...,n \qquad (5)$$
$$x_i^* = (g_w z_w^* - \gamma_w^*)/(f_i q_w); i=1,2,...,m$$

By duality the production frontier for unit j=1,2,...,N satisfies

$$\alpha^{*\prime} Y_j \le \alpha_0^* + \beta^{*\prime} X_j + \gamma^{*\prime} Z_j; (\alpha^*, \beta^*, \gamma^*) \ge 0$$

where the equality holds if unit j is efficient and there is no degeneracy due to congestion costs. Clearly a negative (positive or zero) value of α_0^* implies increasing (diminishing or constant) returns to scale.

Note that this generalized quadratic programming model (3) has many flexible features compared to the traditional DEA model (2). First of all, if the research inputs are viewed as cumulative stream of past investment as in Arrow model of learning by doing, then the cost function TC in (3) may be viewed as a long run cost function. Given the capital input z* the reference firm solves the optimal current inputs x_i^* through minimizing the short run cost function $TC(x|z^*)$. Second, the learning effect parameter $f_i > 0$ shows that the efficiency estimates through DEA model (2) would be biased if it ignores the learning parameters. Third, the complementarity (i.e., interdependence) of the two types of inputs is clearly brought out in the linear relation between x_i^* and z_w in (5). For example, it shows that

$$\partial x_i^* / \partial z_w^* > 0, \partial x_i^* / \partial f_i > 0, \partial x_i^* / \partial \beta_i^* > 0$$
and
$$\partial z_w^* / \partial x_i^* > 0, \partial z_w^* / \partial f_i > 0, \partial z_w^* / \partial \gamma_w^* > 0$$

Finally, compared to a linear program this quadratic programming model (3) permits more substitution among the inputs, thus making it possible for more units to be efficient.

One limitation of the long run cost (3) minimization model above is that it ignores the time profile of output generated by cumulative investment experience. Let $z(t) = (z_w(t))$ be the vector of gross investment and $k(t) = \int_0^t z(s)ds$ be the cumulative value where

$$\dot{k}_w(t) = z_w(t) - \delta_w k_w(t) \qquad (6)$$
δ_w : fixed rate of depreciation

In this case the transformed DEA model becomes dynamic as follows:

$$\text{Min} \int_0^\infty e^{-\rho t} \left[c'(t)x(t) + C(z(t)) \right] dt$$

subject to (6) and the constraints of model (2)

Here $C(z(t))$ is a scalar adjustment cost, which is generally assumed nonlinear in the theory of investment. This type of formulation has been recently analyzed by Sengupta (1999, 2000), which shows the stability and adaptivity aspects of convergence to the optimal path.

Another type of characterization of the research inputs and their productivity is in the current literature of new growth theory. Thus Lucas

(1993) considered a growth process where each firm has a production function, where its output depends on its own labor and physical capital inputs as well as the total knowledge capital of the whole industry. The availability of industry's knowledge capital occurs through the spillover mechanism or diffusion of the underlying information process. The utilization of the industry's knowledge capital by each firm has been called by Jovanovic (1997) as the learning effect, which is very significant in the modern software based industries. To characterize this learning effect we introduce a composite input vector X_j^C for DMU_j as the share of each DMU_j out of the industry total supply of each input, e.g., $\sum_{j=1}^{N} X_{ij}^C = X_i^T$, where X_i^T is the total industry supply of input i. We can then formalize the input-oriented DEA model in two forms as before:

$$\text{Min } \theta + \phi$$
$$\text{s.t.} \quad \sum_{j=1}^{N} X_j \lambda_j \leq \theta X_h; \sum_j X_j^C \lambda_j \leq \phi X_h^C \quad (7)$$
$$\sum_j Y_j \lambda_j \geq Y_h; \lambda'e = 1, \lambda \geq 0$$

and

$$\text{Min } C = c'x + q'x^C$$
$$\text{s.t.} \quad X\lambda \leq x; X^C \lambda \leq x^C; Y\lambda \geq Y_h; \lambda'e = 1; \lambda \geq 0 \quad (8)$$

On using the Lagrange multipliers α, β, γ and α_0, the production frontier for DMU_h in case of model (8) may be easily derived from the dual problem as

$$\alpha'Y_h = \beta'X_h + \gamma'X_h^C + \alpha_0; \alpha, \beta, \gamma \geq 0$$

Clearly the interdependence of the two inputs x and x^C can be easily introduced in this framework through nonlinear interaction terms in the objective function of (8) or, through the method used in (3) before.

Thus the generalized DEA models incorporate three additional sources of relative efficiency not found in the conventional DEA models: (1) unit cost reduction due to the complementarity effect of R&D inputs, (2) the increasing returns to scale due to learning by doing and finally (3) the spillover effect of knowledge capital in the industry as a whole.

Dynamic Cost Frontier

We now consider dynamic cost frontiers with knowledge capital as in the current models of endogenous growth. For this purpose it is convenient to aggregate all inputs into a single cost and relate this cost to a single output in order to derive a cost frontier. Like a dynamic production frontier, a dynamic cost frontier helps to characterize the technological progress associated with the input and output growth. We consider these two aspects in this section.

Consider the production function of a firm with a single output (y) and m inputs (x_i) at time t

$$y = f(x_1, x_2, ..., x_m, t) \tag{9}$$

Let $\dot{A}/A = (\partial f / \partial t)(1/f)$ denote the proportional shift in the production function with time and it is called technological progress (regress), which we wish to relate to the index of productivity. On taking the time derivative of equation (9) and dividing by output one obtains

$$\dot{y}/y = \sum_{i=1}^{m} \frac{\partial f}{\partial x_i} \frac{x_i}{y} \frac{\dot{x}_i}{x_i} + \dot{A}/A \tag{10}$$

where dot denotes the time derivative. Assume that the firm minimizes the total cost (c) for producing y. Then the first order conditions for cost minimization imply $\partial f / \partial x_i = w_i / (\partial c / \partial y)$ where $\partial c / \partial y$ is marginal cost and w_i is the input price of x_i. On using this result in (2) one obtains

$$\dot{y}/y = \sum_{i=1}^{m} \varepsilon^{-1} \frac{w_i x_i}{c} \frac{\dot{x}_i}{x_i} + \dot{A}/A \tag{11}$$

where $\varepsilon = \frac{\partial c}{\partial y} \frac{y}{c}$ is the elasticity of cost with respect to output and $c = \sum w_i x_i$ is total cost of inputs. To aggregate inputs into a single composite input (F) we follow the Divisia index method of aggregation due to Diewert (1976), Denny, Fuss and Waverman (1981) and others where

$$\dot{F}/F = \sum_{i=1}^{m} \frac{w_i x_i}{c} \frac{\dot{x}_i}{x_i} \tag{12}$$

On combining (11) and (12) one obtains

$$\dot{A}/A = \dot{y}/y - \varepsilon^{-1}(\dot{F}/F) \tag{13}$$

Since TFP = y/F, the proportional rate of growth of TFP is

$$\frac{\dot{TFP}}{TFP} = \frac{\dot{y}}{y} - \frac{\dot{F}}{F}$$

A rearrangement of (11), (12) and (13) yields

$$\dot{A}/A = \frac{\dot{TFP}}{TFP} + (1-\varepsilon^{-1})\frac{\dot{F}}{F} \tag{14}$$

or

$$\frac{\dot{TFP}}{TFP} = \frac{\dot{A}}{A} + (\varepsilon^{-1}-1)\frac{\dot{F}}{F} \tag{15}$$

Clearly if there is constant returns to scale then $\varepsilon = 1$ and hence

$$\dot{A}/A = \dot{TFP}/TFP \tag{16}$$

Otherwise the TFP growth rate exceeds (falls short of) the growth rate of A, when there exists increasing (diminishing) returns to scale.

By duality the shift in the production function can be easily related to the shift in the total cost function

$$c = g(w_1, w_2, \ldots, w_m, t) \tag{17}$$

Let $\dot{B}/B = (1/c)(\partial g/\partial t)$ be the proportionate shift in the cost function (9). Then one can show that the upward shift of the production frontier (or productivity growth) is equivalent to the downward shift (or cost efficiency growth) of the cost frontier. For example if we write the cost frontier as $c = By^{\varepsilon-1}$, then $\ln c = \ln B + (\varepsilon-1)\ln y$. On taking the time derivative, one obtains

$$(-\dot{B}/B) = \frac{\dot{TFP}}{TFP} + (\varepsilon - 1)\frac{\dot{y}}{y} \qquad (18)$$

or

$$\frac{\dot{TFP}}{TFP} = -\frac{\dot{B}}{B} + (1-\varepsilon)\frac{\dot{y}}{y} \qquad (19)$$

Denny, Fuss and Waverman (1981) have applied this model to estimate the growth of TFP in Canadian telecommunications industry by assuming a translog cost function in a regression framework. It is clear from (19) that in case of constant returns to scale ($\varepsilon=1$) we have

$$\dot{TFP}/TFP = -\dot{B}/B = \dot{A}/A$$

i.e., technological progress ($\dot{A}/A$) equals the downward shift ($-\dot{B}/B$) of the cost function. Moreover if the production function (9) is log-linear, then it can be specified as

$$\ln c = \ln B + \sum_{i=1}^{m} \tilde{\beta}_i \ln w_i + (1/\sum_{i=1}^{m} \beta_i)\ln y \qquad (20)$$

where $\tilde{\beta}_i = \beta_i / \sum_{i=1}^{m} \beta_i$ and β_i is the elasticity of output with respect to input x_i in the log-linear production function. Clearly the cost elasticity of output is given by $\varepsilon = (\Sigma\beta_i)^{-1}$, where the case of increasing returns to scale yields scale economies, i.e., $\varepsilon < 1.0$. Note that if input price data are available, one can also define an aggregate input F_j.

When input price data are available, these can be utilized in defining an aggregate input F_j for firm j by following the formulation (13) before. Let $\hat{F}_j = \Delta F_j / F_j$ and $\hat{y}_j = \Delta y_j / y_j$ denote the proportional growth rates of input and output for firm j. Then one can test the relative efficiency of firm h by setting up the LP model

$$\text{Min } \phi$$
$$\text{s.t. } \sum_{j=1}^{N} \hat{F}_j \mu_j \leq \phi\hat{F}_h; \sum_{j} \hat{y}_j \mu_j \geq \hat{y}_h \qquad (21)$$
$$\Sigma\mu_j = 1; \mu_j \geq 0; j = 1,2,...,N$$

If firm h is efficient (i.e., $\phi^* = 1.0$ with all slack zero), then this yields the simple production frontier

$$\Delta y_h / y_h = \frac{b^*}{a^*} \frac{\Delta F_h}{F_h} + \frac{b_0^*}{a^*} \qquad (22)$$

where the Lagrangean function is

$$L = -\phi + b(\phi \hat{F}_h - \Sigma \hat{F}_j \mu_j) + a(\Sigma \hat{y}_j \mu_j - \hat{y}_h) + b_0(1 - \Sigma \mu_j)$$

with ϕ, b, a nonnegative and b_0 unrestricted in sign. On comparing (13) and (22) it is easy to deduce that the cost elasticity of output for firm h is $\varepsilon_h^* = a^*/b^*$ and $\Delta A_h / A_h = b_0^*/a^*$, where asterisks denote optimal values. Hence the downward shift of the cost frontier for the efficient firm h can be specified as

$$-\Delta B_h / B_h = \frac{b_0^*}{a^*} + \left(\frac{b^*}{a^*} - 1\right) \frac{\Delta F_h}{F}$$

Clearly if $b^* = a^*$ then $\Delta A_h / A_h = -\Delta B_h / B_h$, i.e., the upward shift of the production frontier equals the downward shift of the cost frontier for the efficient firm h.

Note that by varying h within the set $I_N = \{1,2,\ldots,N\}$ the industry can be decomposed into two groups of firms: one containing the relatively efficient firms and the other comprising nonefficient ones. Two implications of this cost-oriented formulation are important for analyzing the dynamics of a technology-intensive industry such as personal computers or semiconductors. One is the exit behavior of firms, which are not growth efficient, i.e., high host firms fail to survive the competitive pressure. On replacing F_j by its associated cost C_j, the cost frontier for the efficient firm h can also be written as

$$\Delta C_h / C_h = (a^*/b^*)(\Delta y_h / y_h) - b_0^*/b^*$$

When firms are not on this dynamic cost frontier above, competitive pressure crushes them in the long run, i.e., they are more vulnerable to being squeezed out of the market.

A second aspect of this dynamic model is that some types of nonlinearity can be easily built into it. This nonlinearity may reflect the second order effects of output growth on the pattern of input and cost growth. Thus consider the LP model (21) with $\hat{F}_j = \hat{C}_j = \Delta C_j / C_j$ and adjoin the nonlinear constraint

$$\Sigma \hat{y}_j^2 \mu_j = \hat{y}_h^2$$

as an equality so that its Lagrange multiplier α is unrestricted in sign. The cost frontier for the efficient firm h then gets transformed as follows

$$\Delta C_h / C_h = (a^*/b^*)(\Delta y_h / y_h) + (\alpha^*/b^*)(\Delta y_h / y_h)^2 - (b_0^*/b^*)$$

Clearly if α^* is negative, then as output growth rises, the marginal rate of cost falls, i.e.,

$$\partial \hat{C}_h / \partial \hat{y}_h = (a^*/b^*) + 2\alpha^* \hat{y}_h / b^*$$
$$< 0 \text{ if } \hat{y}_h = \Delta y_h / y_h > \frac{-a^*}{2\alpha}$$

In this case the efficient firms would tend to reap the benefits of declining costs at an increasing rate, thus forcing the inefficient firms to exit in the long run.

It is important to point out here that the link of our dynamic cost efficiency approach with the specification by a Malmquist productivity index analyzed in some detail by Sengupta (1995). In this latter approach the productivity index is equivalent to the ratio of two input distance functions for two periods t_1 and t_2. If these distance functions are denoted by D_1 and D_2, then the ratio D_2/D_1 produces a measure of technical progress or regress representing the shift in the input distance function using the input output bundles z_t, for $t = t_1$ and t_2. But since by duality the upward shift of the production frontier is equivalent to the downward shift of the cost frontier, our cost efficiency model represents an equivalent paradigm. The cost efficiency model is more appropriate, since the various input components of R&D expenditure and learning experience cannot be easily separated out.

Next we consider the impact of the input called knowledge capital, which may exhibit the learning phenomena. Let k_j denote the knowledge capital for firm j and c_j be the average cost per unit of output. The efficient firm h seeks to minimize the discounted stream of average production costs in order to determine the optimal levels of costs (inputs) and knowledge capital, when investments (z) lead to the growth of knowledge capital. The decision model then takes the form

$$\text{Min } J = \int_0^\infty e^{\rho t}(c + i(z))dt$$

s.t. $\quad \dot{k} = z(t) - \delta k$ (23)

$$\sum_{j=1}^N c_j \lambda_j \leq c; \sum_j \lambda_j y_j \geq y_h$$

$$\sum_j \lambda_j y_j^2 = y_h^2, \Sigma k_j \lambda_j \leq k$$

$$\Sigma \lambda_j = 1, \lambda_j \geq 0; j = 1, 2, ..., N$$

Here dot over a variable denotes the time derivative, i(z) is the cost of investment and δ is the fixed rate of depreciation. Here the nonlinear output constraint $\Sigma \lambda_j y_j^2 = y_h^2$ is specified in equality form, so that its Lagrange multiplier (a) may be free in sign. Here firm h is tested for overall Pareto efficiency relative to the cluster of N firms in the industry. This type of dynamic model can be easily solved by Pontryagin's maximum principle, where one introduces the Hamiltonian function H as

$$H = e^{-\rho t}[c + i(z) + s(z - \delta k(t))]$$

where s = s(t) is the adjoint function. If the optimal path of knowledge capital k(t) exists, then by Pontryagin's maximum principle there must exist a continuous function s(t) satisfying

$$\dot{s}(t) = (\rho + \delta)s - b \quad (24)$$

where one uses the augmented Lagrangean function

$$L = H + e^{-\rho t}[\beta(c - \Sigma c_j \lambda_j) + \alpha(\Sigma \lambda_j y_j - y_h)$$
$$+ a(\Sigma \lambda_j y_j^2 - y_h^2) + b(k - \Sigma \lambda_j k_j)$$
$$+ \beta_0(\Sigma \lambda_j - 1)]$$

Assuming interior optimal solutions the efficient firm h must satisfy the following necessary conditions, which are also sufficient here:

$$\beta - 1 = 0, \text{ i.e., } \beta = 1$$
$$c_h = \beta_0 + a y_h^2 - b k_h; \, \beta_0 \text{ and a free in sign} \qquad (25)$$
$$\partial i(z)/\partial z = s(t) \text{ at each t}$$

The last condition of (25) states that the marginal investment cost for the efficient firm h must equal the optimal shadow price s(t) for every positive level of investment. If the investment cost is of a quadratic form, i.e., $i(z) = (u/2) z^2$, $u > 0$, then this optimality condition reduces to

$$z(t) = s(t)/u, \text{ hence } \dot{k}(t) = s(t)/u - \delta k(t) \qquad (26)$$

Furthermore, the transversality condition must hold for the dynamically efficient firm:

$$\lim_{t \to \infty} e^{-\rho t} s(t) = 0 = \lim_{t \to \infty} e^{-\rho t} s(t) k(t) \qquad (27)$$

Note that the optimal trajectories or expansion paths {k(t), s(t)} determined by the above system defined by (25)-(27) have several interesting economic implications for efficiency.

First of all, the cost frontier in (25) for the efficient firm shows a decline in average production cost when the level of knowledge capital increases. Furthermore, if the coefficient α is negative, then for higher levels of output $y_h > \alpha/(2|a|)$ the marginal cost may also decline. Secondly, the steady state solution $(\bar{k}, \bar{s})$ on the optimal trajectory would be stable if the following two conditions hold

$$\bar{s}/u \lessgtr \delta \bar{k} \text{ according as } k \gtrless \bar{k}$$

and

$$(\rho + \delta)\bar{s} \lessgtr \bar{b} \text{ according as } s \gtrless \bar{s}$$

since the two differential equations above are linear. Also one could combine the two differential equations, i.e., adjoint equations into a single second order equation

$$u\ddot{k}(t) - u\rho\dot{k}(t) - u\delta(\rho+\delta)k(t) + b = 0 \tag{28}$$

Its characteristic equation is

$$\mu^2 - \rho\mu - \delta(\rho+\delta) = 0$$

which shows the two roots to be real and opposite in sign, i.e., $\mu_1 > 0$, $\mu_2 < 0$. Thus the steady state pair $(\bar{k}, \bar{s})$ has the saddle point property. On assuming a fixed steady state value for b as $\bar{b}$, the transient solution of equation (28) can be written as

$$k(t) = \left[k(0) - \frac{\bar{b}}{u\delta(\rho+\delta)}\right]e^{\mu_2 t} + \frac{\bar{b}}{u\delta(\rho+\delta)}$$

Note that the constant term A_1 in the solution

$$k(t) = A_1 e^{\mu_1 t} + A_2 e^{\mu_2 t} + \frac{\bar{b}}{u\delta(\rho+\delta)}$$

has to be set equal to zero in order to satisfy the transversality condition (27). Finally, if the observed path of accumulation of knowledge capital equals the optimal path over time, then the firm would exhibit dynamic efficiency; otherwise the conditional cost function would exhibit myopic inefficiency.

An Empirical Application

We consider in this section some empirical applications of the LP models developed before to measure economic efficiency in terms of technological progress and efficiency growth. The application here is selective in that not all firms of the computer industry are included here. A more detailed study of this industry has been reported by Sengupta (2002) elsewhere, where the empirical details of the various component costs and the growth in sales are analyzed.

An empirical application to a set of 12 firms (companies) in the US computer industry over a 12-year period (1987-98) is used here to illustrate the concept of dynamic efficiency. The selection of 12 companies is made from a larger set of 40 companies over a 16-year period. R&D input is used here as a proxy for knowledge capital. We have used Standard and Poor's Compustat Database (SIC codes 3570 and 3571) for the input and output data for the 12-year period 1987-98. This selection is based on two considerations: (1) survival of firms through the whole period and (2) promising current profit records. The companies are: Compaq, Datapoint, Dell, Sequent, Data General, Hewlett-Packard, Hitachi, Toshiba, Apple, Maxwell, Silicon Graphics and Sun Microsystems.

The single output variable (y) is net sales in dollars per year and the nine inputs in dollars per year are combined into three composite inputs: x_1 for R&D expenditure, x_2 for net plant and equipment and x_3 for total manufacturing and marketing costs.

We consider input-based level and growth efficiency in terms of non-radial measures of efficiency, i.e., efficiency specific to each input. The level efficiency model is

$$\text{Min} \sum_{i=1}^{3} \theta_i$$
$$\text{s.t.} \quad \sum_{j=1}^{12} y_j \lambda_j \geq y_k; \sum_{j=1}^{12} x_{ij} \lambda_j \leq \theta_i x_{ik}, i = 1, 2, 3 \qquad (29)$$
$$\Sigma \lambda_j = 1, \lambda_j \geq 0; 0 \leq \theta_i \leq 1$$

and it is applied for three years 1987, 1991 and 1998. The growth efficiency model is used in the form

$$\text{Min} \sum_{i=1}^{3} \phi_i$$
$$\text{s.t.} \quad \sum_{j=1}^{12} (\Delta y_j / y_j) \mu_j \geq \Delta y_k / y_k \qquad (30)$$
$$\sum_{j} (\Delta x_{ij} / x_{ij}) \mu_j \leq \phi_i (\Delta x_{ik} / x_{ik}), i = 1, 2, 3$$
$$\Sigma \mu_j = 1, \mu_j \geq 0; 0 \leq \phi_i \leq 1$$

over three year periods 1987-90, 1991-94 and 1995-98. Tables 1 and 2 present the empirical results. It is interesting to observe that a firm which is sequentially level efficient over the three years 1987, 1991 and 1998 is not necessarily growth efficient. Such an example is Hitachi, whose net sales did not grow as fast as some of its competitors.

Measuring technological progress by the shadow price of the constraint $\Sigma \mu_j = 1$ the ranking of the 12 firms appears as follows:

	1987-90 rank		1991-94 rank		1995-98 rank
Datapoint	1	Dell	1	Datapoint	1
Data General	2	Silicon	2	Maxwell	2
Sequent	3			Compaq	3
HP	4			Dell	4
Toshiba	5			Data General	5
Sun	6			Sequent	6
Hitachi	7			Silicon	7
Apple	8				
Compaq	9				
Silicon	10				

Note that during 1991-94 only Dell and Silicon Graphics exhibited positive technological progress, others with zero or negative technological progress. Datapoint regained its first rank during the recent period 1995-98. Table 2 also shows Datapoint to be growth-efficient in terms of all the three inputs over all the periods. On writing the dual formulation of the LP model (30) the dynamic production frontier for the efficient firm k may be written as

$$\alpha^*(\Delta y_k / y_k) = \beta_0^* + \sum_{i=1}^{3} \beta_i^* (\Delta x_{ik} / x_{ik}) \qquad (31)$$

The values of the technological progress ($\beta_0^* > 0$) or regress ($\beta_0^* < 0$) appear as follows:

	1987-90		1995-98
Datapoint	10.74	Datapoint	19.35
Data General	3.32	Maxwell	7.36
Sequent	3.24	Compaq	1.86
Toshiba	0.261	Sequent	0.38
Sun	0.260	Silicon	0.10
Hitachi	0.25		
Apple	0.08		
Compaq	0.40		
Silicon	0.041		

Note that when one divides both sides of (31) by the optimal values of α^*, all the coefficients of input growth become less than one.

Measuring Solow-type technological progress by the ratio β_0^*/α^*, we obtain the following results:

(i) Technological progress is above 4% per year for 58% of firms in 1987-90, 83% in 1991-94 and 75% in 1995-98.

(ii) Some typical examples are (in percents):

1987-90 HPC (6.4), DGC (4.9), DEL (3.8) and SUN (4.9)

1991-94 DGC (5.1), HPC (9.0), APL (9.1) and SIL (6.4)

1995-98 DGC (6.1), HIT (9.0), COM (16.4) and MAX (7.7)

The sum of the input coefficients $\sum_{i=1}^{3} \beta_i$ measuring returns to scale is equal to or exceeds unity in all cases of the sample of efficient firms.

A second way of analyzing the empirical results is to run a regression of the dependent variable log output = $\hat{y}$ on the three independent variables: log R&D ($\hat{x}_1$), log plant and equipment ($\hat{x}_2$) and log cost of goods sold ($\hat{x}_3$) with a dummy variable D for each coefficient, where D = 1.0 for the efficient firms and zero otherwise. The results are as follows:

1987-98 $\hat{y} = 1.199^{**} + 0.162^{**} \hat{x}_1 + 0.065^* D \hat{x}_1$
$+ 0.009 \hat{x}_2 - 0.034 D \hat{x}_2$
$+ 0.743^{**} \hat{x}_3 + 0.034^* D \hat{x}_3$ ($R^2 = 0.996$)

1991 $\hat{y} = 1.214^{**} + 0.262^{**} \hat{x}_1 - 0.075 \hat{x}_2$
$+ 0.791^{**} \hat{x}_3$ ($R^2 = 0.998$)
D significant for $\hat{x}_1$ and $\hat{x}_3$ only

1998 $\hat{y} = 0.925^{**} + 0.140^* \hat{x}_1 + 0.015 \hat{x}_2$
$+ 0.0842^{**} \hat{x}_3$ ($R^2 = 0.998$)
D significant for $\hat{x}_1$ and $\hat{x}_3$ only

Clearly R&D expenditures have played a most dynamic role in the productivity of the efficient firms in the computer industry and this trend is likely to continue in the future.

2.2 Technology and Productivity Growth

Following Schumpeter's dynamic innovation approach D'Aveni (1994) has characterized the competitive high-tech framework as hypercompetition. He argues that this hypercompetitive world has a striking similarity with the Darwinian world of survival of the fittest, where the rival competitors get crushed, if they are not on the leading edge of the production and cost frontier. It is in this framework that one has to distinguish between the *level* and *growth* efficiency. Following Solow (1997) the former characterizes the output level along a production frontier, whereas the latter considers a state of sustained acceleration of growth of output due to a faster rate of technological progress. Growth in the level of technology is exactly what is meant by technological progress. How does technological progress (regress) affect the firms in the high-tech industry? For one thing the entry and exit behavior of firms are strongly influenced by it. Failure to innovate and succeed in the hypercompetitive market may result in firm decay and exit. Secondly, the scale economies and learning curve effects may hasten the sustained growth process for the growth-efficient firms.

Our objective in this section is two-fold. One is to formulate a *nonparametric* model of the production and cost frontier of a high-tech industry, where firms survive in the long run if they maintain both level and growth efficiency. The second objective is to empirically apply this nonparametric model to the US computer industry over a 12-year period 1987-98.

We have discussed in the previous section the relation of technology and productivity and growth. We consider first an input-oriented nonparametric model for testing the Pareto efficiency of a reference firm or unit h in a cluster of N firms, where each firm j produces s outputs (y_{rj}) with m inputs (x_{ij})

$$\text{Min } \theta \text{ subject to } \sum_{j=1}^{N} X_j \lambda_j \leq \theta X_h \qquad (32)$$

$$\sum_{j=1}^{N} Y_j \lambda_j \geq Y_h; \sum_{j=1}^{N} \lambda_j = 1, \lambda_j \geq 0$$

Here X_j and Y_j are the observed input and output vectors for each firm j, where $j = 1,2,\ldots,n$ and λ_j are the nonnegative weights to be optimally determined along with the scalar variable θ. Let (λ^*, θ^*) denote the optimal solutions of the linear programming (LP) model (13) with all slacks zero. Then the reference unit or firm h is said to be *technically efficient* (i.e., production efficiency) if $\theta^* = 1$. If however, θ^* is positive but less than unity, then it is not technically efficient, since it uses excess inputs measured by $(1 - \theta^*)x_{ih}$. Thus, in case of technical or production inefficiency, the first set of (input) constraints shows that a linear convex combination of other firms in the industry does better in using less inputs, while the second set of (output) constraints if it holds with inequality shows that the convex linear combination of other firms does better also in terms of producing more output than the reference firm h.

Note that θ^* here provides a radial measure of technical efficiency in terms of the proportionate reduction of inputs. A more general measure (i.e., a nonradial measure) would replace θ by θ_i (i=1,2,…,m) for each input i and change the objective function θ to $\sum_{i=1}^{m} \theta_i$. Also, an output-oriented efficiency measure ϕ can be easily superimposed, e.g.,

$$\text{Max } \phi - \theta$$
$$\text{s.t. } \sum_j X_j \lambda_j \leq \theta X_h; \sum_j Y_j \lambda_j \geq \phi Y_h$$
$$\sum_j \lambda_j = 1, \lambda_j \geq 0; j = 1,2,\ldots,N$$

Some important uses of the above LP model (32) specifying a free disposal convex hull as the production frontier may now be mentioned. First of all, if there is one output (e.g., composite output) and technical efficiency holds for firm h, then by duality one obtains the linear production frontier

$$y_h = \beta_0^* + \sum_{i=1}^{m} \beta_i^* x_{ih} \qquad (33)$$

where $\beta_i^* = b_i^*/a^*, \beta_0^* = b_0^*/a^*$ with b_i^* and a^* being the optimal dual variables associated with the input and output constraints and b_0^* with the convexity constraint $\Sigma \lambda_j = 1$. If the input parameters β_i^* remain invariant as the inputs and output change, then the production expansion path would appear as

$$\Delta y_h = \Delta \beta_0^* + \sum_{i=1}^{m} \beta_i^* \Delta x_{ih}$$

Now consider the single output version of inputs and outputs in logarithmic units, i.e., model (1) with $\tilde{x}_{ij} = \ln x_{ij}, \tilde{y}_j = \ln y_j$, then the production frontiers above would be transformed as follows

$$\tilde{y}_h = \tilde{\beta}_0^* + \sum_{i=1}^{m} \tilde{\beta}_i^* \tilde{x}_{ih}$$

$$\dot{y}_h / y_h = \dot{A}/A + \sum_i \tilde{\beta}_i^* (\dot{x}_{ih}/x_{ih})$$

where $\tilde{\beta}_0^* = \dot{A}/A$ denotes technological progress (regress) as defined as before in (10). Here $\tilde{\beta}_i^*$ is nonnegative but $\tilde{\beta}_0^*$ is unrestricted in sign due to the convexity restriction $\Sigma \lambda_j = 1$.

A second feature of the LP model (32) is that it identifies the industry into two groups of firms, the technically efficient and the nonefficient ones. If N_1 is the number of efficient firms with $\theta^* = 1$ for each, then $N_2 = N - N_1$ is the total number of inefficient firms with $\theta^* < 1.0$ for each. If the inefficient firms continue to be inefficient for several years, then they may not survive the pressure of competition. This aspect may be more clearly shown, whenever we have observable market price data for the inputs (q_i). In this case the reference firm h seeks to minimize total costs C by selecting the optimal inputs $(x = (x_i))$:

$$\text{Min } C = \sum_{i=1}^{m} q_i x_i$$

s.t. $\sum_{j=1}^{N} X_j \lambda_j \leq x; \sum_j y_j \lambda_j \geq y_h$

$\Sigma \lambda_j = 1, \lambda_j \geq 0; j=1,2,\ldots,N$

Let (x^*, λ^*) be the optimal solution with optimal costs $C^* = q'x^*$. If firm h is efficient in attaining the minimal cost level C^*, then its input vector (X_h) equals x^* and its production frontier becomes

$$y_h = (\beta_0^*/\alpha^*) + \sum_{i=1}^{m} x_{ih}(\beta_i^*/\alpha^*)$$

where the Lagrangean function is

$$L = q'x + \beta'(x - \sum_j X_j \lambda_j) + \alpha(\Sigma y_j \lambda_j - y_h) + \beta_0(1 - \Sigma \lambda_j)$$

Clearly the set (N_2) of inefficient firms has cost levels C_j higher than C^* for each $j=1,2,\ldots,N_2$. If this state $C_j > C^*$ continues for some time, the higher cost firms have to exit from the industry due to competitive pressure of the overall market. In the long run minimizing average cost (AC) rather than total cost may be more appropriate for determining the optimal output (y^*) and the optimal inputs (vector x^*). This yields the following model:

Min $AC = \sum_i q_i x_i / y$

s.t. $\sum_j X_j \lambda_j \leq x; \sum_j y_j \lambda_j \geq y; \Sigma \lambda_j = 1; \lambda_j \geq 0$

On using the Lagrangean expression

$$L = AC + \sum_{i=1}^{m} \beta_i(x_i - \sum_j X_j \lambda_j) + \alpha(\sum_j y_j \lambda_j j - y) + \beta_0(1 - \Sigma \lambda_j)$$

the optimal scale of output (y^*) and the corresponding input vector (x^*) may be determined from the following production frontier relations

$$\alpha^* y_j = \beta_0^* + \sum_i \beta_i^* x_{ij}; j \text{ efficient}$$

and

$$y^* = q_i / \beta_i^* = (\sum_i q_i x_i^* / \alpha^*)^{1/2}$$

Let c_0 denote the minimum average cost when the optimum scale of output is y* determined as above. If market demand curve is $Y = D(p)$, then the perfectly competitive equilibrium price is $p = c_0$ and the corresponding equilibrium output is $Y^e = D(p^e) = D(c_0)$. The size of the total market (S) may then be determined by the ratio of the competitive output to the optimum scale, i.e., $S = Y^e/y^*$. Thus following the limit pricing theory the inefficient firms having average costs higher than c_0 would tend to exit in the long run.

Another feature of the nonparametric model (32) is that the subset of efficient firms can be separately tested and discriminated at the second stage. Thus let N_1 be the set of technically efficient firms determined at the first stage. Let i be a specific input representing R&D or knowledge capital, which embodies new technology. Then at the second stage we ask how many of the efficient firms utilize this critical input most efficiently? For this purpose we set up the LP model

$$\text{Max } E_{ih} = \sum_{r=1}^{s} u_{irh} y_{rh} / x_{ih}$$

$$\text{s.t. } \sum_{r=1}^{s} u_{irh} y_{rj} \leq x_{ij}; j = 1, 2, ..., N \quad (34)$$

$$u_{irh} \geq \varepsilon_0; r = 1, 2, ..., s$$

where ε_0 is a small positive number in order to ensure a positive optimal value of the weight u_{irh} attached to output r when evaluating the efficiency of input i of firm h=1,2,…,N. Here E_{ih} denotes the efficiency score of input i for the reference firm h. The interpretation of the efficiency score in the LP model (34), where x_{ij} and y_{rj} are the observed inputs and outputs is very simple. For example assume that a firm h uses two inputs (i=1,2) and has a score of 0.7 in relation to input 1 and 0.8 for input 2, this means it could aim to maintain the same outputs as before but using only 70% of the current level of input 1 and 80% of the current level of input 2. If instead we consider increasing output levels, then based on input 1 the outputs are currently 30% below the optimal value and 20% below in relation to input 2. Thus if we do not wish to raise input levels, then we can choose the lower of these two figures for calculating optimal target outputs, we could then make some savings on input 1.

Now we consider a growth efficiency model analogous to model (32) but using one output and m inputs. Let $\hat{X}_j = \dot{x}_{ij}/x_{ij} = \Delta x_{ij}/x_{ij}$ and $\hat{y}_j = \dot{y}_j/y_j = \Delta y_j/y_j$ denote the proportional rates of growth of observed inputs and outputs μ_j be the nonnegative weight for firm j. Then the nonparametric growth efficiency model solves for each reference firm h the optimal values of δ and μ as follows:

Min δ

s.t. $\sum_{j=1}^{N} \hat{X}_j \mu_j \leq \delta \hat{X}_h ; \sum_j \hat{y}_j \mu_j \geq \hat{y}_h$ (35a)

$\Sigma \mu_j = 1, \mu_j \geq 0; j = 1, 2, ..., N$

If the reference firm h is efficient, then $\delta^* = 1.0$ and the production frontier takes the form

$$\dot{y}_h / y_h = \gamma_0^* + \Sigma \gamma_i^* (\dot{x}_{ih}/x_{ih})$$

where γ_0^* is unrestricted in sign and the other γ_i^*'s are nonnegative. For finite increases we have

$$\Delta y_h / y_h = \gamma_0^* + \sum_i \gamma_i^* (\Delta x_{ih}/x_{ih})$$ (35b)

with $\gamma_0^* = \Delta A/A$ denoting technological progress when positive and technological regress when negative. For high-tech industries such as computers or telecommunications the input and output growth may be measured, e.g., as a four-year average and then the technological progress (regress) estimated over a 12-year period. If a firm has the value $\delta^* = 1.0$ for each of the three subperiods, then its growth efficiency is persistent and the values of γ_0^* are most likely to be positive. In case of inefficient firms these conditions would fail to hold. Thus if a firm h is efficient (i.e., $\theta^* = 1.0$) in terms of the level efficiency model (32), it may not be growth efficient ($\delta^* = 1.0$) in terms of the model (35a). Furthermore by considering, e.g., four year average growth rates of inputs and outputs one could estimate the long run changes in the technology parameter $\gamma_0^*(\tau)$, where τ denotes a 4-year subperiod, e.g., if $\gamma_0^*(1) > \gamma_0^*(2) > \gamma_0^*(3)$ then the technological progress is increasing.

With panel data on the observed inputs and outputs of firms the level efficiency model (32) may be used in two other ways. One is to consider the subset of efficient firms only over a period T and run a loglinear regression of outputs on the inputs as in (17) and test if the regression coefficients are significantly different from the subset of inefficient firms. Secondly, the sources of change in $\tilde{\beta}^*(t)$ over t=1,2,...,T may be analyzed by a regression model with other exogenous and independent variables such as growth of international demand or expansion in government research expenditures.

The growth efficiency model (35a) can also be utilized for asking the above two questions but time series data over a much longer period would be needed. One important aspect of the growth process, e.g., learning by doing may be more easily specified in this framework. Thus assume that each input x_i improves over time due to experience and its value changes to $v_i x_i$ with $v_i \geq 1$. This means that the production function $y = (x_1, x_2, ..., x_m)$ changes to $y = f(v_1, x_1, v_2, x_2, ..., v_m x_m)$. In Arrow's learning by doing model the first input is capital (x_1), which measures cumulative gross investment $x_1(t) = \int_{-\infty}^{t} I(r)dr$ as cumulative experience and the second input (x_2) is labor which is augmented as $v_2 x_2$ where $v_2 = x_1^b$. In the general case all the inputs may improve due to the accumulation of experience. In order to incorporate this idea we adjoin into the growth model (35a) a new set of restrictions as

$$\sum_{j=1}^{N} \mu_j \frac{\Delta v_{ij}}{v_{ij}} \leq \delta \frac{\Delta v_{ih}}{v_{ih}} \tag{36}$$

This yields for the efficient firm h a new growth frontier as

$$\frac{\Delta y_h}{y_h} = \gamma_0^* + \sum_{i=1}^{m} \gamma_i^* \frac{\Delta x_{ih}}{x_{ih}} + \sum_{i=1}^{m} g_i^* \frac{\Delta v_{ih}}{v_{ih}} \tag{37}$$

where g_i^*'s are the optimal values of the Lagrange multipliers associated with the constraints (35). Thus the production frontier (37) exhibits increasing returns to scale due to $\Sigma g_i^* > 1$ even when $\Sigma \gamma_i^* = 1.0$. In recent models of endogenous growth theory 'knowledge capital' has been identified with this type of increasing returns to scale. Recently Solow (1997) has considered an extended version of Arrow's learning by doing model, where there is increasing returns to scale to cumulative investment alone. In new growth theory Lucas (1993) considered a growth process where each firm has a production function, where its output depends on its own labor and physical capital inputs as well as the total knowledge capital of the whole industry. The availability of industry's knowledge capital occurs through the diffusion of the underlying information process. The utilization of the industry's knowledge capital has been called by Jovanovic (1997) as the learning effect, which plays a very significant role in the modern microelectronic and computer industries. To characterize this learning effect we introduce a composite input vector x_j^c for firm j as the share of firm j out of the industry total supply of each strategic input k. We then adjoin a new set of constraints for each k as

$$\sum_{j=1}^{N} \hat{X}_j^c \mu_j \leq r\hat{X}_h^c$$

with a modified objective function: Min $\delta + r$, where $\hat{X}_j^c = (\Delta x_{kj} / x_{kj})$. The production frontier for the efficient firm h incorporates in this case the impact on output growth due to the industry spillover effect:

$$\frac{\Delta y_h}{y_h} = \gamma_0^* + \sum_{i=1}^{m} \gamma_i^* \frac{\Delta x_{ih}}{x_{ih}} + \sum_{k=1}^{m} \tau_k^* \frac{\Delta x_{kh}^c}{x_{kh}^c}$$

Recently Norsworthy and Jang (1992) have empirically shown for the semiconductor and computer industries in US the significant effect on output growth due to this knowledge spillover mechanism throughout the industry as a whole. In models of hypercompetitive markets D'Aveni (1994) has characterized this spillover effect as *'access efficiency'*, i.e., the access to industry's knowledge capital, which improves productivity and reduces unit costs.

Empirical Application to Computer Industry

Empirical applications to a set of 22 firms (companies) in the computer industry in US over a 12 year period (1987-98) are attempted here by way of illustrating the concepts of level and growth efficiency developed in the earlier section. The selection of 22 companies is from a larger set of 40 companies over a 16-year period 1984-99. Since a large number of smaller firms did not survive over the whole period and some input data are unavailable for some years, we had to restrict to 22 firms over the period 1987-98. Standard and Poor's Compustat Database (SIC Code 3570 or 3571) provides the main source of input and output data. As outputs two variables are selected: y_1 for net sales revenue realized for electronic computer goods at the time of delivery or shipment and y_2 for other incomes from various other related transactions. In the one output case only the sales variable is used, since it corresponds more closely to net operating revenue from sales of electronic computers. Nine inputs are selected from the Compustat Database representing both financially related input variables such as manufacturing costs and marketing costs and also "net capital employed" at the end of the reporting period representing input variables such as working capital, plant and equipment and other fixed assets. Three inputs in manufacturing costs are x_1 for all supplies, materials and related costs, x_2 for labor and related expenses inclusive of pension and retirement expenses and x_3 for all direct overhead expenses including amortization of deferred costs, maintenance and repair costs and also customer sponsored research and development expenses. Three inputs related to marketing costs include x_4 for advertising costs, x_5 includes such activities as (a) company sponsored or purchased research and development, (b) software development expenses and (c) amortization of software costs for companies that recognize software revenues. Net capital employed in current dollars includes x_7 for working capital (which represents the difference between total current assets minus total current liabilities as reported on a company's balance sheet), x_8 for net property plant and equipment and x_9 for other fixed assets. The net plant and equipment variable x_8 includes such items as (a) the book value of fixed assets sold, (b) sale of fixed assets and (c) the transfer of property, plant and equipment to inventory accounts. Of all the nine input variables, four are most important from an economic viewpoint, e.g., x_2 as labor costs, x_4 for advertising, x_5 for R&D expenses and x_8 for net plant and equipment. The production frontiers (33) and (35b) for the efficient firms exhibit through the parameters β_2^* and γ_2^* the contribution of labor productivity, while β_5^* and γ_5^* show the impact of R&D on output growth. Advertising expenditure reflects in some sense the pressure of market competition for capturing demand. Recent studies of hyper-competition have emphasized that significant scale economies in demand provide a major source of competitive pressure in the network economy.

Moreover, we have to note that the growth of the computer industry over the recent decade has not only changed the inter-firm structure of the industry itself, but also affected significantly the productivity growth in other industries, which are using more and more the information technology of the computer industry. Thus the recent empirical study by Jorgenson and Stiroh (2000) noted two effects on overall growth of the US economy resulting from massive increases in computer power currently experienced in US. First, as the production of computers improves and becomes more efficient, more computing power is being produced from the same inputs, i.e., learning by doing. This increases the overall productivity in the computer-producing industry and contributes to TFP growth for the economy as a whole. Labor and R&D productivity also grow at both the industry and the aggregate levels. Secondly, the computer-using industries are now using skilled labor working with more and better computer equipment and this investment increased labor productivity in these industries. They noted that the industry productivity growth (i.e., TFP growth in a specific industry) over the period 1958-96 was the highest in two high-tech industries: (a) industrial machinery and equipment, and (b) electronic and electric equipment at 1.5 percent and 2.0 percent per year respectively. Note that the industrial machinery and equipment includes the production of computer equipment, while electronic and electric equipment includes the production of semiconductors and communications equipment. Enormous technological progress in the production of these high-technology capital goods has generated productivity growth and falling prices. For instance, average computer prices declined by 18 percent per year from 1960 to 1995 and by 27.6 percent per year over 1995-98.

Two broad groups of empirical applications are attempted here for the microcomputer industry comprising 22 firms (companies) over the period 1987-98. The companies included here comprise some of the well-known firms as Apple, Compaq, Dell, IBM, Gateway, and HP and also lesser-known firms such as AST Research, Fujitsu, Toshiba and Maxwell. Due to a variety of differentiated products we had to use net sales revenue as a single output measure (y) when we had to use a one output model for the production frontier. The first group of applications deals with the measurement of level efficiency as discussed in equation (32), while the second group analyzes the measurement of growth efficiency and technological progress as discussed before.

Tables 3-5 show two features of level efficiency as measured by model (32) with one output (y_1) and nine inputs. One is that more than one-third of computer firms (i.e., 35% on average) has remained below the production frontier on the average for the whole period. This is so inspite of the fact that demand growth has proceeded at a very high rate exceeding 15 percent per year. The average rate of return on all assets for the computer industry as a whole have increased from an annual rate of 31.1% to 34.5% over the period 1975-84 according to Norsworthy and Jang's estimate. Also the average computer prices have declined by 18% per year form 1960 to 1995 according to Jorgenson and Stiroh's estimate. Secondly, the major source of inefficiency measured by the positive value of $(1 - \theta^*)$ has been the inefficient utilization of the R&D expenses, which has a very significant contribution on the output growth. When TFP growth is measured from the time series estimates of the intercept term in the production frontier in logarithmic form (e.g., Table 4), the efficient firms perform much better than the inefficient ones. Table 5 shows very clearly through the application of the one input model (34) involving the R&D input that even some of the efficient firms (e.g., HP in 1991, 1998) are not always utilizing the R&D input most efficiently relative to other firms.

The growth efficiency estimates in Tables 6-7 show very clearly the very high and steady growth in technological progress among the growth-efficient firms. Thus average technological growth ($\Delta \bar{A} / \bar{A}$) rose from 16.1% in 1987-89 to 25.4% in 1993-95 and to 27.8% in 1996-98. Another major feature has been the sustained increase in RTS (return to scale). For the computer industry as a whole including both the mainframe and microcomputers this feature has been empirically substantiated by Norsworthy and Jang (1992). Their regression estimates from a translog cost function found RTS to be around 1.400 for the period 1973-80, though in recent years this may have declined slightly.

Table 7 shows that in terms of technological progress and R&D efficiency the growth efficient firms have outperformed the inefficient ones to a significant degree. This is also borne out by the regression estimates in Table 8, which show output growth in terms of the growth of individual inputs. Once again technological progress and the research input (x_5) turn out to be highly significant in a statistical sense. When a nested regression model with dummy variable D is used, the difference between the growth-efficient and inefficient firms turns out to be statistically significant.

Thus our empirical estimates tend to confirm two broad results. First, growth efficiency measures are more sensitive than the level efficiency. The impact of scale economies (RTS) and TFP growth is more distinctively borne out by the growth efficiency estimates. Secondly, the microcomputer industry has to undergo a most rapid shift in technological change due to the most intense competition pressure as revealed by the steep decline in average computer prices. This calls for developing new theoretical models of hypercompetition based on the experiences of the technology-intensive computer industry.

Table 1. Non-radial measures (θ_i^*) of level efficiency

	1987			1991			1998		
	R&D (x_1)	Net plant (x_2)	Total prod. cost (x_3)	x_1	x_2	x_3	x_1	x_2	x_3
Data General	0.55	0.15	1.0	1.0	1.0	1.0	0.59	0.58	1.0
HP	1.0	1.0	1.0	1.0	1.0	1.0	1.0	1.0	1.0
Hitachi	1.0	1.0	1.0	1.0	1.0	1.0	1.0	1.0	1.0
Toshiba	1.0	1.0	1.0	1.0	0.96	0.97	1.0	1.0	1.0
Apple	1.0	1.0	1.0	1.0	1.0	1.0	0.40	0.69	1.0
Compaq	1.0	1.0	1.0	1.0	1.0	1.0	1.0	1.0	1.0
Datapoint	0.62	0.20	0.97	1.0	1.0	1.0	1.0	1.0	1.0
Dell	1.0	1.0	1.0	1.0	1.0	0.94	1.0	1.0	1.0
Maxwell	1.0	1.0	1.0	1.0	1.0	1.0	1.0	1.0	1.0
Sequent	1.0	1.0	1.0	1.0	1.0	1.0	0.64	0.53	1.0
Silicon Graphics	0.38	0.52	0.70	1.0	1.0	1.0	0.51	0.71	1.0
Sun Microsystems	0.57	0.29	1.0	1.0	1.0	1.0	1.0	1.0	1.0

Table 2. Non-radial measures (θ_i^*) of growth efficiency

	1987-90			1991-94			1995-98		
	x_1	x_2	x_3	x_1	x_2	x_3	x_1	x_2	x_3
Data General	1.0	1.0	1.0	1.0	1.0	1.0	0.48	0.54	0.77
HP	0.49	1.0	0.47	0.55	0.80	1.0	1.0	1.0	1.0
Hitachi	0.40	0.68	0.65	1.0	1.0	1.0	0.94	0.84	1.0
Toshiba	0.29	0.62	0.72	1.0	1.0	1.0	1.0	1.0	1.0
Apple	0.52	0.69	0.64	0.51	0.44	0.76	1.0	1.0	1.0
Compaq	0.40	0.54	0.50	1.0	1.0	1.0	0.33	0.60	0.75
Datapoint	1.0	1.0	1.0	1.0	1.0	1.0	1.0	1.0	1.0
Dell	0.61	0.44	0.47	1.0	1.0	1.0	1.0	1.0	1.0
Maxwell	1.0	1.0	1.0	1.0	1.0	1.0	1.0	1.0	1.0
Sequent	1.0	1.0	1.0	1.0	1.0	1.0	0.50	0.54	0.48
Silicon Graphics	1.0	1.0	1.0	1.0	1.0	1.0	0.25	0.25	0.38
Sun Microsystems	1.0	1.0	1.0	1.0	1.0	1.0	0.42	0.24	0.67

Table 3. Level Efficiency in Computer Industry
(Selected years)

	No. of firms inefficient	Average efficiency score (θ^*)	Main source of inefficiency
1987	8/22	0.82	R&D (x_5)
1989	7/22	0.90	R&D (x_5)
1991	9/22	0.92	Adv. Expense (x_4)
1993	10/22	0.95	Plant & Equip (x_8)
1995	7/22	0.92	R&D (x_5)
1998	6/22	0.94	R&D (x_5)

Table 4. Average Efficiency Scores of Efficient and Inefficient Firms

	Efficient		Inefficient	
	$\bar{\theta}^*$	$\Delta\bar{A}/\bar{A}$	$\bar{\theta}^*$	$\Delta\bar{A}/\bar{A}$
1987	1.0	-	0.82	-
1989	1.0	0.194	0.90	1.44
1991	1.0	0.221	0.92	0.138
1993	1.0	0.212	0.95	0.152
1995	1.0	0.215	0.92	0.149
1998	1.0	0.219	0.94	0.151

Note: Median value of efficiency score and TFP growth are denoted by $\bar{\theta}^*$ and $\Delta\bar{A}/\bar{A}$ respectively.

Table 5. Efficiency in Utilization of the R&D Input Among Selected Firms
(two outputs and one input)

	1987		1991		1995		1998	
	OE (overall efficiency)	R&D efficiency	OE	R&D	OE	R&D	OE	R&D
Toshiba	87	91	85	90	86	89	83	85
Gateway	100	100	100	96	98	100	100	100
Dell	100	100	100	98	95	98	97	98
HP	97	96	100	96	96	99	100	98
IBM	90	91	91	89	92	89	94	95
Compaq	85	97	89	85	91	85	90	81

Table 6. Average Growth Efficiency of Efficient and Inefficient Firms over Selected Subperiods

	Efficient firms		Inefficient firms	
	$\Delta\bar{A}/\bar{A}$	RTS (returns to scale)	$\Delta\bar{A}/\bar{A}$	RTS
1987-89	0.161	1.04	0.062	0.75
1990-92	0.192	1.07	0.071	0.78
1993-95	0.254	1.09	0.103	0.79
1996-98	0.278	1.10	0.082	0.76

Selected firms	$\Delta\bar{A}/\bar{A}$	RTS
Toshiba		
1987-89	0.10	0.89
Gateway		
1996-98	0.08	0.91
1987-89	0.14	1.08
1996-98	0.26	1.03
Dell		
1987-89	0.19	1.12
1996-98	0.25	1.05
Compaq		
1987-89	0.12	0.94
1996-98	0.15	0.91

Table 7. Sources of Growth Efficiency

	Technological Progress (%)		R&D efficiency (%)		Labor input (%)	
	87-91	93-98	87-91	93-98	87-91	93-98
A. Efficient firms	26	31	28	29	30	32
B. Inefficient firms	15	17	17	19	21	24

Note: The percentage contributions of inputs are averages for respective periods.

Table 8. Regression Estimates of Output Growth of an Average Growth-efficient Firm
(based on models (26) and (28))

Dependent Variable	Parameter estimates							
	γ_0^*	γ_2^*	γ_4^*	γ_5^*	γ_8^*	g_5^*	R^2	
$\Delta y_h/y_h$	0.092 (t=2.51)	0.061 (2.71)	0.021 (1.81)	0.101 (3.45)	0.005 (1.01)	0.092 (2.10)	0.95	Eq. (26)
	b^*/a^*	b_0^*/a^*	R^2					
$\Delta y_h/y_h$	1.05 (3.12)	0.12 (2.98)	0.97					Eq. (28)
	γ_0^*	$D\gamma_0^*$	γ_2^*	$D\gamma_2$	γ_5^*	$D\gamma_5^*$	R^2	
$\Delta y_h/y_h$	0.089 (t=2.34)	0.024 (6.45)	0.051 (2.43)	0.002 (4.56)	0.124 (3.91)	0.001 (6.24)	087	

Note: D is a dummy variable with a value 1.0 if the observed firm is growth efficient, zero otherwise.

References

- Charnes, A., Cooper, W.W., Lewin, A., Seiford, L., (1994): Data Envelopment Analysis. Kluwer Academic Press, Boston
- D'Aveni, R.A. (1994): Hypercompetition: Managing the Dynamics of Strategic Maneuvering. Free Press, New York
- Denny, M., Fuss, M., Waverman, L. (1981): The Measurement and Interpretation of Total Factor Productivity in Regulated Industries, with an Application to Canadian Telecommunications. In: Cowing, T.G., Stevenson, R.E. (eds.), Productivity Measurement in Regulated Industries. Academic Press, New York
- Diewert, E.W. (1981): The Theory of Total Factor Productivity Measurement in Regulated Industries. In: Cowing, T.G., Stevenson, R.E. (eds). Productivity Measurement in Regulated Industries. Academic Press
- Farrell, M.J. (1957): The Measurement of Productive Efficiency. Journal of Royal Statistical Society 120, 253-290.
- Fried, H.O., Lovell, C., Schmidt, S. (eds.) (1993): The Measurement of Productive Efficiency. Oxford University Press, Boston
- Jorgenson, D.W., Stiroh, K.J. (2000): Raising the Speed Limit: US Economic Growth in the Information Age. In: Brainard, W.C., Perry, G.L. (eds.), Brookings Papers on Economic Activity. Brookings Institution, Washington, DC
- Lucas, R.E. (1993): Making a Miracle. Econometrica 61, 251-272
- Jovanovic, B. (1997): Learning and Growth. In: Kreps, D.M., Wallis, K.F. (eds.), Advances in Economics and Econometrics. Cambridge University Press, Cambridge
- Hall, R.E. (1990): Invariance Properties of Solow's Productivity Residual. In: Diamond, P. (ed.), Growth, Productivity and Unemployment, MIT Press, Cambridge
- Norsworthy, J.R., Jang, S.L. (1992): Empirical Measurement and Analysis of Productivity and Technological Change. North Holland, Amsterdam
- Sengupta, J.K. (2000): Dynamic and Stochastic efficiency Analysis: Economics of Data Envelopment Analysis. World Scientific, Singapore
- Shapiro, C., Varian, H.L. (1999): Information Rules: A Strategic Guide to the Network Economy. Harvard Business School Press, Boston
- Solow, R.M. (1997): Learning from Learning by Doing: Lessons for Economic Growth. Stanford University Press, Stanford

3
Cost Oriented Efficiency

The theory and applications of data envelopment analysis (DEA) have mostly used observed input output data to compare the relative efficiency of firms or decision-making units (DMUs) in an industry or organization. The cost output relations of firms and the overall industry behavior have been either ignored or very infrequently analyzed. As a result the influence of the overall market on the cost efficiency of firms and the dynamics of entry and exit behavior of firms under varying efficiency and demand fluctuations have rarely been looked into.

Our object here in this chapter is three fold. One is to introduce a cost oriented DEA model, with costs depending on outputs and capital inputs. Cost frontiers are then specified in two forms: short run and long run, where the capital inputs are absent (present) in the short (long) run. Secondly, overall demand conditions and their fluctuations are introduced here through a two-stage model. In the first stage, inter firm comparisons are made through DEA models to specify the cost frontier as a strictly convex function of outputs and capital inputs. In the second stage we minimize total industry costs under the condition that total industry supply meets total market demand. This determines an equilibrium price in the competitive industry comprising efficient firms. Finally, the changes in price are analyzed through a dynamic adjustment process due to entry or exit of firms in the industry. This framework of analysis provides a general equilibrium transformation of the DEA model, which only treats a partial equilibrium setup.

3.1   Data Envelopment Analysis

The simplest form of a cost oriented DEA model is to compare the observed total cost C_h of a firm (DMU) h in relation to other firms in the industry. Let C_j and C_j^* be the observed and optimal cost of output y_j for firm j=1,2,...,n where $C_j \geq C_j^*$ and let $C_j^* = b_0 + b_1 y_1 + b_2 y_j^2$ be the convex cost frontier with all parameters positive. To test the relative cost efficiency of firm h we set up the linear programming (LP) model

$$\text{Min } \varepsilon_h = C_h - C_h^*$$
$$\text{subject to} \quad b_0 + b_1 y_j + b_2 y_j^2 \leq C_j; j = 1, 2, ..., n \qquad (1)$$

The dual of this model can be easily derived as the standard input-oriented form

$$\text{Min } \theta$$
$$\text{s.t.} \sum_{j=1}^{n} C_j \lambda_j \leq \theta C_h; \sum_{j=1}^{n} y_j \lambda_j \geq y_h; \Sigma y_j^2 \lambda_j \geq y_h^2 \qquad (2)$$
$$\sum_{j=1}^{n} \lambda_j = 1; \lambda_j \geq 0 \text{ for } j = 1,2,\ldots,n$$

Let (λ_j^*, θ^*) be the optimal solution of (2) with all slack variables zero. If $\theta^* = 1.0$ then firm h is on the cost frontier, i.e., $C_h = C_h^*$. But if $0 < \theta^* < 1$, then there exists a convex combination of costs of other firms such that $\Sigma \lambda_j^* C_j < C_h$, i.e., firm h is not on the cost efficiency frontier. Clearly when the firm h is not on the cost efficiency frontier one may adjust its cost C_h by replacing it with $\theta^* C_h$ where $0 < \theta^* < 1$ and then the adjusted cost output data of firm h would belong to the cost frontier. By varying h over the index set $I_n = \{1,2,\ldots,n\}$ one can thus obtain the whole cost frontier.

The total costs above include both variable and fixed costs. But if we separate fixed costs and specify the cost function as $C_j = C_j(y_j, k_j)$, where k_j is capital inputs (fixed cost), then we may modify the LP formulation by adding the following constraints

$$\sum_{j=1}^{n} k_j \lambda_j \leq k_h; \sum_{j=1}^{n} k_j^2 \lambda_j = k_h^2 \qquad (3)$$

of which the second constraint is imposed as an equality in order to maintain the strict convexity of the cost function $C_j(y_j,k_j)$ with respect to k_j.

Note that the LP model (3) specifies the long run efficiency model (LREM), when the capital inputs used by each firm j are observed and therefore the cost function C_j depends on both output and capital inputs. Since capital inputs are more durable, one may easily build here a dynamic adjustment process over time as follows: at period t, firm j has a capital endowment $k_j(t-1)$ inherited from period t-1; it decides to invest (disinvest) in period t so as to reduce the cost of using existing capacity in the production of optimal output $y_j^*(t)$. Thus one obtains in period t the level of capital inputs as

$$k_j(t) = f(k_j(t-1), y_j^*(t)), j = 1, 2, ..., n \qquad (4)$$

This yields a system of difference equation in $k_j(t)$:

$$k_j(t) = u_j + v_j k_j(t-1) \qquad (5)$$

if the function $f(\cdot)$ is assumed to be linear. Note that the parameters u_j, v_j of the capital adjustment equation may be related to the process of learning by firms in their dynamic optimization decision, which may be specified separately. Thus by changing k_j, k_h by $k_j(t-1)$ and $k_h(t-1)$ and using (5) one may build a dynamic process of long run adjustment along the cost frontier.

The short run efficiency model (FREM) is given by the LP model (2), where the capital inputs are all fixed and given and hence total costs depend only on outputs. Now consider a cost efficient firm j as specified by (2). It is on the cost frontier

$$\beta C_j = \beta_0 + \alpha_1 y_j + \alpha_2 y_j^2$$

which yields

$$C_j = \gamma_0 + \gamma_1 y_j + \gamma_2 y_j^2$$

where $\gamma_0 = \beta_0/\beta, \gamma_i = \alpha_i/\beta, i = 1, 2 \qquad (6)$

where the parameters are nonnegative. In particular we need $\gamma_2 > 0$ for strict convexity and $\gamma_0 > 0$ for the U-shaped average cost curve which is normally used in production literature.

The convex cost frontier (6) for an efficient firm j has two important implications when the overall market facing each firm is perfectly competitive. In this framework firms are price takers and the equilibrium price clears the market. The dynamics of price and quantity adjustment in this overall market may be easily analyzed in this framework by a Walrasian process. This aspect will be analyzed later. A second implication is that the firm size for each firm based on its production technology may be easily specified in the minimum efficient scale (MES). Since average cost $c_j = C_j/y_j$ derived from (6) is twice continuously differentiable on $(0,\infty)$ and strictly U-shaped with minimum attained at $y_j^* \in (0,\infty)$, hence $AC(y_j^*)$ is strictly convex and $MES(y_j^*) > 0$ for each efficient firm j. Thus $MES(y_j^*)$ for (6) is given by $y_j^* = (\gamma_0/\gamma_2)^{1/2}$.

If all firms have identical technology and in the long run firms can choose plant size (i.e., k_j) and enter or leave the market (i.e., free entry and free exit), then the cost frontier (6) already incorporates optimal adjustment in capacity and hence the long run average cost LRAC(y*) may be written as

$$LRAC(y^*) = \gamma_1 + 2\sqrt{\gamma_0 \gamma_2}$$

Let $Y^* = \Sigma y_j^*$ be total industry output and $p = F(Y^*)$ be the price given by the inverse demand function. Then the long run perfectly competitive equilibrium results in aggregate output Y^* and equilibrium price $p = F(Y^*)$ such that

$$F(Y^*) = LRAC(y^*)$$

with each active firm operating the optimally efficient plant size at output y* and earning zero profits, where normal returns are included in the economic concept of profit here. Clearly if

$P > F(Y^*)$, new firms enter

or $p < F(Y^*)$, old firms exit

This result has two significant implications at an applied level. One is for the profit oriented firms in the private sector. The long run dynamics of the entry and exit behavior for the whole industry may be easily modeled here. Assuming continuous adjustment the Walrasian process of disequilibrium may be specified in a linear form as follows:

$$dY^*/dt = a(p - LRAC(y^*))$$
$$dp/dt = b(D(p) - Y^*) \qquad (7)$$

where D(p) is the market demand function $D(p) = F^{-1}(Y)$ and the positive parameters a, b reflect the respective speeds of adjustment for the aggregate quantity and price. At equilibrium we obtain $p^* = LRAC(y^*)$ and $D(p^*) = Y^*$.

A second applied implication is that the market demand function $F(Y^*) = LRAC(y^*) = p$ can be empirically estimated for different industries and their impact on $LRAC(y^*)$ of individual firms through the entry-exit dynamics can be worked out. For example if price falls due to a fall in demand, e.g., declining exports or recession in other sectors, then this will accentuate the rate of potential exit.

For the public sector firms the profit basis of the entry-exit behavior would not hold. However setting price equal to $LRAC(y^*)$ provides a natural rule of optimal pricing when $LRAC(y^*) = LRMC(y^*)$, where $LRMC(y^*)$ denotes the long run marginal cost. Any administered price above or below $LRAC(y^*)$ would be inoptimal, since it would yield outputs different from $MES(y^*)$.

3.2 Industry Equilibrium

When the capital inputs (k_j) are specifically introduced into the cost function $C_j(y_j, k_j)$ the industry equilibrium may be derived into two ways. One is to use the allocative efficiency version of the DEA model and solve for the long run market equilibrium in two stages. Given market price $\hat{p}$ and the capital inputs $\hat{k}_j$, the first stage maximizes profit with respect to output:

$$\pi_j = \hat{p}\, y_j - C_j(y_j, \hat{k}_j) \tag{8a}$$

This determines optimal output y_j^* and hence total output Y^*. The second stage solves the problem

$$\max \pi_j = \hat{p}\, y_j^* - C_j(y_j^*, k_j) \tag{8b}$$

by choosing optimal capital inputs k_j^* and hence the aggregate capital inputs $K^* = \Sigma\, k_j^*$ are determined. The aggregate demand function $F(Y^*)$ then determines the equilibrium price p^*. For the extended DEA model specified by (2) and (3) the cost frontier for firm j is

$$C_j = \tilde{\gamma}_0 + \tilde{\gamma}_1 y_j + \tilde{\gamma}_2 y_j^2 - b_1 k_j + b_2 k_j^2 \tag{9}$$

Equation (8) then yields the optimal output

$$y_j^* = (\hat{p} - \tilde{\gamma}_1)/(2\tilde{\gamma}_2), \text{ i.e., } \hat{p} = MC_j(y_j^*)$$

whereas optimal capital inputs are given by (9) as $k_j^* = b_1/(2b_2)$. The equilibrium price p* is then determined by the condition that total supply Y* equals total demand D(p*).

In the second case we apply the capital decision problem as one of dynamic optimization subject to an investment path followed by each firm. For example if z_j is gross investment and δ is the constant rate of depreciation the dynamics of investment may be specified as

$$dk_j/dt = z_j - \delta k_j \tag{10}$$

and each firm may choose the optimal path of k(t) by minimizing the discounted cost of capital

$$\text{Min} \int_0^\infty e^{-rt} C_j(y_j^*, k_j(t)) dt \tag{11}$$

subject to the dynamic condition (10) above. Note that this dynamic optimization problem replaces the static problem (9) above.

So far we have assumed that all firms have identical technology but firms may have different AC functions in competitive equilibrium. Two approaches may be adopted in such a situation. The first is due to Novshek (1980) who suggested a method of transformation to generate a family of AC functions indexed by α. This transformation changes the scale of measurement of output as follows: for each $\alpha \, \varepsilon (0, \infty)$, the α-size firm corresponding to AC is the firm AC_α defined by $AC_\alpha(y) = AC(y|\alpha)$. With this transformation one can assume that any basic AC function has MES equal to one and use $\alpha > 1$ to generate the other AC functions with different MES, i.e., $AC_\alpha(y) = \alpha C(y|\alpha)$ where $C(\cdot)$ is the total cost function. With this transformation we obtain as before the perfectly competitive equilibrium price p* = AC(y*) and D(F,AC(y*)) = Y*, where F is the inverse demand function.

The second approach is due to Dreze and Sheshinski (1984), who assume that each firm j belongs to one of M possible types of cost functions and that n_j is the number of firms of type j. In the first stage each firm tries to be on the cost frontier (6) but in the second stage of industry equilibrium we seek to minimize total industry costs

$$TC = \sum_{j=1}^{M} n_j C_j(y_j)$$

$$\text{s.t.} \quad \sum_{j=1}^{M} n_j y_j \geq D; \ y_j \geq 0 \tag{12}$$

here $D = D(p)$ is total industry demand and $Y = \Sigma\, n_j y_j$ is total industry supply. Let p be the Lagrange multiplier for the demand supply constraint in (12). Kuhn-Tucker conditions for optimal y_j^* and n_j^* then yield

$$MC_j(y_j^*) = p, \ y_j^* > 0$$

$$AC_j(y_j^*) = p, \ n_j^* > 0 \tag{13}$$

where $MC_j(y_j^*) = \gamma_1 + 2\gamma_2 y_j^*$ is marginal cost. Hence

$$p^* = \min AC_j(y_j^*) \tag{14}$$

On using the demand supply equilibrium condition (12) one may easily derive

$$P^* = (D + B)/A$$

where

$$A = \sum_{j=1}^{n} 1/\gamma_{2j}, \quad B = \sum_{j=1}^{n} (\gamma_{1j}/\gamma_{2j})$$

Clearly if A rises, i.e., γ_{2j} falls then cost efficiency improves through declining MC_j and hence price falls. If market demand D falls (rises), other things being equal, equilibrium price falls (rises). Finally, if B rises (falls) due to increase (decrease) of γ_{1j}, then equilibrium price rises (falls).

Two important implications of the relation (14) have to be noted. First of all, the equilibrium price p* is derived here through the market clearing condition. Two stages of this equilibrium process have to be distinguished. In the first stage each firm seeks to attain the cost efficiency frontier. The second stage screens the cost efficient firms by minimizing total industry costs subject to the condition that total industry supply equals or exceeds total market demand. Secondly, one may interpret the equilibrium condition (14) in terms of entry and exit behavior, e.g.,

(i) If $p \geq LRAC_{min}$, the firm should produce y*, y* being the output satisfying (14).

(ii) If $p < LRAC_{min}$, the firm should leave the market.

Thus

$$dn_j / dt = \alpha(p - LRAC_{min}), \alpha > 0 \tag{15}$$

Thus, if $p < LAC_{min}$, then there is exit and if $p > LAC_{min}$, then there is potential entry. It is also possible to derive a direct relationship between the market price p* in (14) and the optimal size of plant measured by $k_j^* = b_1/(2b_2)$, where the cost frontier is given by (9).

Since $dLRAC(y_j)/dy_j = (LRMC_j - LRAC_j)/y_j$, there are three stages according as the left hand size is negative (DRS), positive (IRS) or zero (CRS) indicating diminishing, increasing or constraint returns to scale. The optimal price in (14) specifies the MES, i.e., the most efficient scale of plant.

The equilibrium equations (14) and (15) are helpful in capturing the impact of competitive pressure in the overall market, which has been recently characterized as hypercompetition. Models of hypercompetition recently analyzed by Sengupta (2002a) show that increasing returns to scale and dynamic efficiency improvements through innovations play a critical role, when the overall market is on the upswing or downswing depending on the state of economy as a whole. For example if price p falls due to a downturn in the overall economy, only the most efficient firms will survive, i.e., the survival of the most fit principle holds. Thus at any given time we may arrange the minimum average cost denoted by c_j in an ascending order

$$c_{(1)} \leq c_{(2)} \leq \ldots \leq c_{(k)}; k \leq n \tag{16}$$

Equilibrium price would then obtain as follows.

Thus $p_{(1)} = c_{(1)}$ would for example be the low cost efficient firm and $p_{(k)} = c_{(k)}$ the high cost efficient firm. When market demand is very low, e.g., $D = D_{(1)}$ at which $p_{(1)}$ only holds, then only the least cost efficient firms survive. When demand is much higher, e.g., $D = D_{(k)}$ then the price $p_{(k)} > p_{(1)}$ can be sustained and the low cost firms would earn rent in the form of excess profit $\Delta\pi = (p_{(k)} - p_{(1)}) y_{(1)} > 0$. Sometimes this least cost price $p_{(1)} = c_{(1)}$ may be due to specific innovations, e.g., specific software development in the computer industry, or to large investments in R&D in prior years.

Let h_t denote the curve in year t of joining points $(y_{(j)}^t, c_{(j)}^t; j=1,2,\ldots,k; t=1,2,\ldots,T)$. The time series data of h_t would then measure how the structure of average costs in relation to output changes over time. This would provide an inter-firm comparison of LRAC changes over time for industries, which are highly cost sensitive due to changes in technology, e.g., microelectronics, computers and bioengineering. The proportion $q_{(1)} = n_{(1)}/n$ of firms with the least average cost $c_{(1)}$ provides an important measure of inter-industry efficiency. Its trend over time indicates if the overall industry is improving (declining) in efficiency.

Empirical Application

In order to indicate the usefulness of the cost efficiency concepts developed here, it is worthwhile to illustrate their application to the computer industry in US. Growth and efficiency in the US computer industry over the period 1985-2000 have been analyzed by Sengupta (2002b) elsewhere. Here our object is to select ten out of 22 companies from the earlier study and apply DEA models to estimate MES for three selected years 1987, 1990 and 1997. The data set is from Standard and Poor's Compustat databank. The total costs comprise the following input costs: R&D expense, cost of goods sold which includes manufacturing, marketing and all administrative costs and the change in inventory costs and finally the cost of plant and equipment net of depreciation. The last item, i.e., net plant and equipment expenditure may be considered as fixed costs, although other fixed overheads like building and property etc. are excluded here. Hence we have to note that about 70% of overall total cost is included here. For the output measure 'net sales' data are used, but these are not deflated, since there is no suitable price index for such a heterogeneous product as computer hardware and related services. Earlier studies by Norsworthy and Jang (1992) covering the period 1959-81 followed a similar procedure to measure output by net sales.

However in order to determine the cost frontier of an efficient firm we adopt a nonradial measure of efficiency, which differs from a radial measure modeling in (2). To test the cost efficiency of firm h we set up the LP model as

$$\text{Min} \sum_{i=1}^{3} \theta_i$$

s.t.
$$\sum_{j=1}^{n} C_{ij}\lambda_j \leq \theta_i C_{ih}; i = 1, 2, 3$$

$$\sum_j y_j \lambda_j \geq y_h \quad (17)$$

$$\sum_j y_j^2 \lambda_j \geq y_h^2$$

$$\Sigma \lambda_j = 1; \lambda_j \geq 0, j = 1, 2, ..., n$$

By using $C_j = \sum_{i=1}^{3} \beta_i C_{ij}$ as the total cost measure where β_i's are the shadow prices of the first three constraints of (17), one could derive the cost frontier specified by (6) before. Since total cost here includes the bulk of fixed costs, $LRAC(y^*) = \gamma_1 + 2\sqrt{\gamma_0 \gamma_2}$ can be directly estimated here. A set of selected estimates is presented in Tables 1-3 at the end. These estimates are only illustrative, since the sample size is very small and there exist outliers in the data, which have not been corrected. Nevertheless two broad results are indicated. First of all, the MES levels of output are significantly higher than the optimal level on the cost frontier. This suggests that dominant firms have a comparative advantage in the long run due to their capacity utilization. Of the three individual cost components (not reported here) the R&D expenditure turns out to be very important along with net plant and equipment expenditure. Secondly, there is wide diversity in MES in the set of 10 companies over the period covered here. Apple Computer seems to have the best cost structure at the end of 1980s and the beginning of 1990 but after 1995 the company had troubles in its marketing policy. The effects can be seen in the changes in optimal average costs and also in its relative ranking in cost efficiency scale. The period of study included the upswing in the US computer industry; competition was intense but the total demand was high enough so that most of the companies survived. However companies like Dell with a better cost structure were able to gain increased market share due to competitive pricing based on MES. This shows the empirical validity of the survivor technique first proposed by Stigler (1958) and recently applied by Rogers (1993), who hypothesized that only the scale efficient size plants in a competitive industry will survive in the long run and their market share would increase over time. In the downswing also these MES plants will survive due to their superior efficiency in terms of minimum average costs.

Implications of Demand Fluctuations

Demand fluctuations that affect optimal capacity utilization can be analyzed in DEA models of industry equilibrium in three interrelated ways. First of all, if market prices of output are available, their fluctuations may reflect demand uncertainty. The allocative efficiency models of DEA are designed to analyze this type of problem, see e.g., Sengupta (2000). A second way is to adjoin a probabilistic demand supply constraint in the DEA model and specifically allow for shortages and inventories as in production scheduling model, e.g., HMMS model. The third approach to be followed here is to introduce an estimated or forecast demand $\hat{d}_j$ for each firm and assume that each firm follows the decision rule

$$DR_1 : y_j = \hat{d}_j \tag{18}$$

The estimated demand $\hat{d}_j$ is obtained from the observed demand $\tilde{d}_j$, which is assumed to follow a fixed probability distribution with mean $\bar{d}_j$ and variance σ_j^2. By using the decision rule DR_1 from (18) the cost frontier equation (2) can be written as

$$C_j = \gamma_0 + \gamma_1 \hat{d}_j + \lambda_2 \hat{d}_j^2$$

Since C_j is strictly convex in $\hat{d}_j$, one can derive by Jensen's inequality

$$EC_j > C_j(\bar{d}_j)$$

Also the expected average cost defined as $EC_j / \bar{d}_j$ is minimized at

$$\bar{y}_j = \bar{d}_j = (\sigma_j^2 + \gamma_0 / \gamma_2)^{1/2}$$

whereas the expected output level (y_j^0) at which the average expected cost is minimized is

$$y_j^0 = d_j^0 = (\gamma_0 / \gamma_2)^{1/2}$$

Clearly $\bar{y}_j > y_j^0$ is due to demand variance being positive. Since σ_j^2 is zero in a deterministic model, the expected capacity output $\bar{y}_j$ is higher than the deterministic capacity output y_j^0 and hence $AC_j(\bar{y}_j) < AC_j(y_j^0)$. If marginal cost $MC_j(\bar{y}_j)$ equals $AC_j(\bar{y}_j)$, then for the deterministic model $AC_j(y_j^0)$ is greater than $MC_j(\bar{y}_j)$ at the expected capacity output. Hence there is economies of scale and the number of firms tends to increase (or the share of the dominant firms increases) till we reach the most optimal expected capacity output at which the competitive equilibrium price p* equals $AC_j(\bar{y}_j) = MC_j(\bar{y}_j)$. The process of entry eases and the industry reaches its equilibrium.

If however we assume that the first efficient firm j is unable to follow the decision rule DR_1, then inventories $(y_j > \tilde{d}_j)$ or shortages $(y_j < \tilde{d}_j)$ may occur and expected inventory and shortage costs have to be included in the total cost data C_j used in the DEA model (2). If only the costs of positive inventory are included in costs, the decision rule (18) may be changed to

$$DR_2 : y_j = \bar{d}_j - q\sigma_j; q = F^{-1}(u_j) \tag{19}$$

where u_j is the probability of the chance constraint $u_j = \text{Prob}(y_j \geq \tilde{d}_j)$ and $F(\cdot)$ is the cumulative distribution function of random demand. Hence one can specify the transformed cost frontier in the stochastic case as

$$C_j^S = \gamma_0 + \gamma_1(\bar{d}_j + q\sigma_j) + \gamma_2(\bar{d}_j + q\sigma_j)^2$$

Compared to the deterministic case C_j^D with $\sigma_j = 0$ we obtain

$$C_j^S \lessgtr C_j^D \text{ as } q \lessgtr 0$$

In the theory of chance-constrained linear programming the decision rule DR_1 is called the first order decision rule. DR_2 incorporates the variance of demand. Higher order decision rules, which incorporate higher moments of the demand distribution, can be similarly incorporated.

This decision rule approach however does not use the concept of industry equilibrium used in (12) in a deterministic framework. A stochastic analogue of model (12) for incorporating the fluctuations in total demand $\tilde{D}$ is more satisfactory in a theoretical sense. This is because the assumption of uncertain demand $\tilde{D}$ incorporates the uncertainty of market demand due to exogenous factors such as the state of the economy, the external global demand and new innovations.

To consider the stochastic transformation of the model (2) we consider an exponential loss function $L = \exp(\alpha \tilde{C})$, where $\tilde{C}$ is the total cost function with induced randomness due to random output (or demand) and α is the constant rate of absolute risk aversion ($\alpha > 0$). Then we consider the model

$$\text{Min EL} = \sum_{j=1}^{M} n_j EL(y_j)$$

$$\text{s.t.} \quad \sum_{j=1}^{M} n_j y_j \geq \tilde{D}; y_j \geq 0$$

where E is expectation. This is equivalent to

$$\text{Min} J = \sum_{j=1}^{M} \left[n_j \left\{ EC_j + (\alpha/2) \text{Var} C_j \right\} \right]$$

s.t. $\Sigma n_j y_j \geq \tilde{D}; y_j \geq 0$ \hfill (20)

where Var(·) denotes the variance. The optimal conditions (13) now become

$$E\ MC_j(y_j^*) = \gamma_1 + 2\gamma_2 \bar{y}_j + (\alpha/2)\ \partial \text{Var} C_j / \partial y_j = \bar{p}$$
$$E\ AC_j(y_j^*) = EC_j + (\alpha/2)\ \text{Var} C_j / \bar{y}_j = \bar{p} \tag{21}$$

with $y_j^*, n_j^* > 0$. If the rate of risk aversion (α) is zero, then we obtain for expected price $\bar{p}$.

$$\bar{p}^* = \min E\ AC_j(y_j^*) = \gamma_1 + 2\sqrt{\gamma_0 \gamma_2}$$

With a positive rate of risk aversion the equilibrium market-clearing price $\bar{p}^*$ would be higher since Var C_j is strictly convex in y_j. Hence MES would be different in a stochastic framework. Note that the explicit solution of the nonlinear model (21) has to be obtained by a convex programming algorithm. If the rate of risk aversion α varies for different j, then similar risk classes indexed by α_j may have to be constructed and then the concept of risk averse efficiency suitable for reach class can be applied e.g., Sengupta (2000) has considered DEA models of portfolio efficiency for mutual fund investments.

General Implications

Some general implications of the transformed DEA models developed here may be presented now in order to show their link to the operations research literature. First of all, the two-stage efficiency models have been explicitly considered by Athanassopoulos and Thanassoulis (1995), where the first stage is formulated in terms of the standard input or output oriented DEA models and the second stage introduces market efficiency, i.e., the ability of a unit to attract customers on demand. In our approach the second stage introduces industry equilibrium, where only the most efficient firms survive. Similarly, Norman and Stoker (1991) compared the performance of 45 manufacturing units in terms of two efficiency scores, e.g., step one score is the standard input-oriented DEA score, while step 2 score involves output or revenue growth. For high-tech industries such as the computer industry over the boom period 1990-2000 output growth due to increase of global demand growth resulted in intense competitive pressure to reduce costs and this phenomena can be more appropriately modeled by a dynamic cost frontier as follows:

$$\text{Min } \theta$$

$$\text{s.t.} \sum_{j=1}^{n} \lambda_j (\Delta c_j / c_j) \leq \theta (\Delta c_h / c_h)$$

$$\sum_{j=1}^{n} \lambda_j (\Delta y_j / y_j) \geq \Delta y_h / y_h$$

$$\sum_{j=1}^{n} \lambda_j (\Delta k_j / k_j) \leq \Delta k_h / k_h$$

$$\sum_j \lambda_j = 1; \lambda_j \geq 0; j = 1, 2, ..., n$$

If firm j is efficient with $\theta^* = 1.0$, then one can derive from the dual:

$$\Delta c_j / c_j = \gamma_0 + \gamma_1 (\Delta y_j / y_j) - \gamma_2 (\Delta k_j / k_j)$$

where $\gamma_1, \gamma_2 \geq 0$, γ_0 free in sign.

Here c_j is average cost and k_j is capital inputs per unit of output. Growth of capital inputs leads to a decline in the average cost ratio and this yields a decline in equilibrium price. If γ_0 is negative, then the dynamic cost frontier exhibits technological progress in the sense of a backward shift of the cost frontier. Much of the investment in capital inputs in the computer industry has taken the form of investment R&D and knowledge capital. Thus Norsworthy and Jang (1992) have empirically found for the period 1958-86 a productivity growth rate of 2 percent per annum, while for the recent period it has exceeded 2.5 percent per year on the average over 1990-2000.

Along with this rapid growth in efficiency in the computer industry, the variance of average costs has increased. This has hastened the process of exit (or declining market share) of firms that could not remain on the dynamic cost frontier.

A second aspect of the cost efficiency models developed here is that the dynamics of the industry model (7) can be analyzed separately from the micro formulation of the DEA model. For example of if r is the eigenvalue of the coefficient matrix in (7), then the characteristic equation can be written as

$$r^2 + g_1 r + g_2 = 0 \tag{22}$$

where $g_1 = a\hat{c} - b\hat{d}$, $g_2 = ab(1 - \hat{c}\hat{d})$, $\hat{c}$ is minimum average cost and $\hat{d}$ the slope of the demand function.

Equation (22) has roots with negative real parts if and only if $g_1 = 0$ and $g_2 > 0$. But if $\hat{d} < 0$ and $\hat{c} > 0$ then these conditions hold and the convergence to equilibrium price p* is assured. However other cases are possible when $\hat{c} < 1/\hat{d}$ yielding two real solutions of (22) one positive and one negative. The equilibrium is then one of saddle point.

Thus the dynamics of price movement for the industry model may affect the allocative efficiency measures of the individual firms and this two-way process of interaction provides an interesting line of new research.

Table 1. DEA Estimates of the Quadratic Cost Frontier (1987)

Company	γ_0	γ_1	γ_2	AC	MES
1. Apple	0.03	0.54	0.01	0.58	1.69
2. Compaq	0.03	0.57	0.0002	0.59	>2.19
3. Datapoint	0.03	0.54	0.01	0.58	1.69
4. Dell	0.03	0.57	0.0001	0.59	>3.25
5. HP	0.05	0.55	0.01	0.60	2.18
6. Hitachi	1.50	0.55	0.01	0.46	11.89
7. Silicon Graphics	0.08	0.26	0.02	0.34	2.05
8. Sun Microsystems	0.03	0.57	0.0001	0.59	>3.10
9. Maxwell	0.03	0.538	0.011	0.58	1.68
10. Encore	0.07	0.258	0.021	0.35	2.04

Notes: 1. The sign > in MES column indicates an estimate greater than the specified output, since γ_2 takes a very small value.
2. Due to rounding the columns AC and MES may not agree with the parametric estimates.

Table 2. DEA Estimates of the Quadratic Cost Frontier (1990)

Company	γ_0	γ_1	γ_2	AC	MES
1. Apple	0.03	0.54	0.01	0.57	2.11
2. Compaq	0.02	0.54	0.0001	0.59	>2.90
3. Datapoint	0.05	0.52	0.0004	0.54	>1.89
4. Dell	0.02	0.59	0.00002	0.59	>4.98
5. HP	0.04	0.55	0.01	0.58	2.21
6. Hitachi	0.004	0.55	0.01	0.56	>0.48
7. Silicon Graphics	0.02	0.59	0.0001	0.59	>14.12
8. Sun Microsystems	0.02	0.59	0.0002	0.59	>10.11
9. Maxwell	0.05	0.51	0.0003	0.55	>12.81
10. Encore	0.02	0.59	0.0002	0.59	>10.05

Note: Comments in footnote of Table 1 apply here also.

Table 3. DEA Estimates of the Quadratic Cost Frontier (1997)

Company	γ_0	γ_1	γ_2	AC	MES
1. Apple	0.02	0.65	0.0002	0.66	>10.20
2. Compaq	0.02	0.60	0.01	0.63	2.00
3. Datapoint	0.02	0.65	0.0001	0.66	>14.14
4. Dell	0.02	0.60	0.01	0.63	2.0
5. HP	0.001	0.60	0.0001	0.62	>10.02
6. Hitachi	0.002	0.42	0.0001	0.44	>20.01
7. Silicon Graphics	0.02	0.65	0.0002	0.66	>10.02
8. Sun Microsystems	0.02	0.60	0.01	0.62	2.01
9. Maxwell	0.02	0.62	0.0002	0.66	>10.15
10. Encore	0.02	0.64	0.0001	0.67	>14.14

Note: Comments in footnote of Table 1 apply here also.

References

- Athanassopoulos, A., Thanassoulis, E. (1995): Separating Market Efficiency from Profitability and its Implications for Planning. Journal of the Operational Research Society 46, 20-34
- Dreze, J., Sheshinski, E. (1984): On Industry Equilibrium Under Uncertainty. Journal of Economic Theory 33, 88-97
- Norman, M., Stoker, B. (1991): Data Envelopment Analysis: The Assessment of Performance. John Wiley, New York
- Norsworthy, J.R., Jang, S.L. (1992): Empirical Measurement and Analysis of Productivity and Technological Change. Amsterdam, North Holland
- Novshek, W. (1980): Cournot Equilibrium with Free Entry. Review of Economic Studies 47, 473-486
- Rogers, R.J. (1993): The Minimum Optimal Steel Plant and the Survivor Technique of Cost Estimation. Atlantic Economic Journal 21, 30-37
- Sengupta, J.K. (2000): Dynamic and Stochastic Efficiency Analysis. World Scientific, London
- Sengupta, J.K. (2002a): Model of Hypercompetition. International Journal of Systems Science 33, 669-675
- Sengupta, J.K. (2002b): Growth and Efficiency in the Computer Industry. Mimeographed paper
- Stigler, G.J. (1958): The Economies of Scale. Journal of Law and Economics 1, 54-71

4
Competition and Efficiency

The foundation of the belief in the desirability of competitive markets derives from the impact of competition on economic efficiency. Economic efficiency can be defined in terms of *Pareto improvement* at three different levels, i.e., efficiency in distribution, efficiency in production and the efficiency in coordination of production and consumption for the whole economy. A feasible allocation vector (x,y) of the consumption vector x = (x_i) for each consumer i and a production vector y = (y_j) for each producer j is defined to be Pareto efficient (or Pareto optimal) if there is no other feasible allocation which is a Pareto improvement on (x,y). The first basic theorem of welfare economics states that a competitive equilibrium is a Pareto optimum. The second basic theorem states that any Pareto optimum can be realized as a particular competitive equilibrium under fairly general conditions i.e., with each Pareto optimum one can associate a price system and a system of resource ownership which would attain, as a competitive equilibrium, this particular Pareto optimum.

This chapter relates the concept of firm efficiency to competitive industry equilibrium. Thus the microtheory of production and allocative efficiency is linked with the efficiency of competitive equilibrium. Competition has been most intense in recent times in some of the new technology-based industries such as microcomputers, telecommunications and bioengineering firms. Declining prices and costs, accelerating global demand and increasing innovation and access efficiency have intensified the competitive pressure in these industries resulting in an environment marked by increasing intra-firm variance in sales and stock market values. Following Schumpeter's dynamic innovation approach D'Aveni (1994) has characterized this state as hypercompetition. He argues that this hypercompetitive world resembles in many ways the Darwinian world of survival of the fittest, where the rival competitors get crushed, if they are not on the leading edge of the innovation efficiency frontier generating sustained price cost efficiency relationships.

Besides the innovation efficiency as the prime mover of growth of firms so strongly emphasized by Schumpeter, three other dynamic forces driving the hypercompetitive markets have been explicitly recognized in the recent literature. The first is the creation of dynamic intra- and inter-industrial externalities by the introduction of *'knowledge capital'* due to information technology. Recent work by the economists in the area of endogenous growth theory, e.g., Romer (1990), Lucas (1993), Jovanovic (1997) and

Sengupta (1998) have emphasized the role of learning by doing and its technological diffusion in the dynamics of industrial growth. In hypercompetition this type of knowledge diffusion is called *'access efficiency'* or *network externalities*. Thus firms pushing for access efficiency race up the escalation ladder in the strongholds area by aggressively competing in the information network of knowledge capital.

The second dynamic force is the demand-side economies of scale, which generates a strong positive feedback in today's information economy. Shapiro and Varian (1999) have strongly emphasized this aspect. They argued for example by using the case of Microsoft's dominance today. This dominance is based on the demand side economies of *scale*. The customers of Microsoft value its operating systems because they are widely used in the industry. Unlike the supply side economies of scale, the demand side economies of scale do not dissipate or get exhausted when the market gets large enough. In static competition cost or price reduction is the major strategy to increase customer demand but in dynamic competition the demand side economies of scale may generate substantial demand shift to higher levels. Clearly this hypercompetitive world may not always be in equilibrium.

The third dynamic force is the creation of new strategic assets by firms in an industry. This has been called *the dynamic resourcefulness* of the innovating firms in hypercompetitive economy by Thomas (1998) and others. This view holds that competition has two faces: static and dynamic. The former takes technology as given, so firms compete only on price and costs. Thus greater competition reduces prices and/or raises costs, thus reducing profits and depreciating assets. In the limit some firms may have to exit due to large depletion of cash flows from dwindling strategic assets. The dynamic or Schumpeterian competition however changes technology at various points of the value chain, thus challenging firms to compete in new innovating ways. Thus the successful firms in an industry transform their technologies so as to create new strategic assets, which bring them new streams of increased cash flow. Thus competition can bring new benefits or increased losses to a firm depending on whether it is mainly static or dynamic.

Our object in this section is to develop a dynamic model of hypercompetition suitable for the technology-intensive sectors of the Internet economy, which is sometimes referred to as the *new economy*. Three features distinguish the new economy from the old. One is the dynamic competition as opposed to the static. This means that *growth efficiency* rather than *level efficiency* is more important for the new economy. Secondly, the three new areas of efficiency central to hypercompetition are: innovation efficiency, access efficiency and resource efficiency. These three constitute the most important forces of dynamic efficiency, which is much different from the production and allocative efficiency underlying static competition. The sources of dynamic efficiency may be better understood if we view the efficiency as an escalation ladder, where the firms grow in dynamic efficiency by racing up the ladder. Thus racing up the escalation ladder in the arena R&D investment, know-how and developing new processes, products and software constitutes *innovation efficiency*. Firms generate new knowledge, e.g., new software, but that knowledge quickly diffuses. This undermines the positions of incumbent competitors, but the next round of innovations gives new or existing competitors an opportunity to seize the initiative.

Access efficiency involves racing up the escalation ladder in the strongholds arena. By building barriers around a stronghold the firms reap monopoly profits in a protected market that can be used to fund aggressive price strategies, R&D investments and other actions. Porter (1987) identifies six major barriers to entry that the firms use to create and sustain a stronghold; dynamic economies of scale, product differentiation, capital requirements, switching costs, access to distribution channels and specific cost advantages like the ownership of low-cost sources of raw materials, favorable locations or government subsidies. Dynamic models of limit pricing discussed by Gaskins (1971), Milgrom and Roberts (1982) and Sengupta (1998) provide only a few aspects of this access efficiency. Finally, the dynamic resourcefulness of firms involving the creation of new strategic assets at various points of the value chain generates resource efficiency. This has been called racing up the escalation ladder in the deep pockets area by D'Aveni (1994). Companies seek to find the best use for their resources or assets even going over to a global setting. Hypercompetitive firms must use their assets to build their next temporary advantage before their competitors. For example, IBM bet the company on the 360 series computers and the bet paid off in the 1960s. But it could not sustain the position because it failed to keep up a strong position in the next temporary advantage, e.g., the personal computer market. Instead tiny companies such as Apple and Microsoft became giants by seizing the next advantage. Thus rivalry between firms in hypercompetition creates pressure on companies to improve and innovate new assets/resources, to lower costs and create new products and processes through new strategic assets. In static competition escalation rivalry lowers the average value of firms in an industry and the intra-industry variance in performance will be small. But in the hypercompetitive world of dynamic competition the rivalry will increase the average firm value at least initially due to the so-called 'creative destruction process' of Schumpeter generating new strategic assets and the intra-industry variance in performance will become larger. This contrasting result: high mean with high variance in hypercompetition and low mean with low variance in traditional static competition may be empirically used to test the persistence of hypercompetition in an industry.

The new economy has another remarkable characteristic in the form of expanding markets, e.g., e-commerce, e-trade. The Internet economy allows the market to expand globally, also intensifying the pressure of competition, which ensures the survival of the fittest ones. Three aspects of this demand explosion are important here. One is the increase in volume of demand due to globalization of trade. Adam Smith who stressed the point that the economies of division of labor is limited by the size of the market had strongly favored the role of international trade and its expansion as the prime mover of industrial growth. The second is the economies of scale in demand rather than supply, which underlies much of industrial expansion in the Internet economy. Shapiro and Varian (1999) has emphasized this point as one of the fundamental information rules for the Internet economy.

Our objective here is two-fold. One is to formalize a model of dynamic economic efficiency in order to illustrate the pattern of growth and decay of firms competing in a hypercompetitive market system. The second is to use the tool of data envelopment analysis (DEA), whereby the growth strategy of successful firms is presented in terms of an escalation ladder of efficiency. Three types of dynamic efficiency in the form of innovation efficiency, access efficiency and resource efficiency are introduced here as the key forces of growth or survival.

4.1 Growth Frontier

Growth and decay of firms in a hypercompetitive market are driven essentially by efficiency (E). This efficiency may be viewed in the context of static competition (E_s) and dynamic competition (E_h), where the latter specifies the state of hypercompetition. Efficiency in static competition (E_s) comprises the technical or production efficiency and allocative or price efficiency. Efficiency in hypercompetition (E_h) has three components: innovations efficiency, access efficiency and resource efficiency. The dynamic nature of efficiency in hypercompetition may involve changes over time in both technical and allocative efficiencies, through a shift in the production frontier or the optimal expansion paths.

Those firms, which cannot sustain dynamic efficiency over time, lag behind in terms of the E_h frontier and as a consequence they feel the pressure to exit. On the other hand, those firms keeping up on the dynamic efficiency frontier tend to gain footholds and grow in market share.

Note that the underlying model here is a demand driven model of cost efficiency; hence it basically specifies a dynamic cost frontier model incorporating the hypercompetitive efficiency strategy. Here average cost (AC) tends to decline due to efficiency improvement and the latter is helped by demand growth, i.e.,

$$d AC/dt = f(\dot{E}_h) \tag{1}$$

$$\dot{E}_h/E_h = f(\dot{D}/D) \tag{2}$$

where the first equation specifies the cost and hence price declines over time due to increase in efficiency, where innovations and access efficiency play the active roles. The second equation specifies Adam Smith's principle of efficiency improvement due to increased market demand and hence increased supply. Secondly, the access efficiency component of E_h involves tacit pro-monopolistic strategies in order to sustain the stronghold arena. It moves the dynamic limit pricing strategy one step further by reducing the price-cost gap in a dynamic setting so that potential entry can be either averted or postponed.

To be more specific consider the growth efficiency frontier for firms, which are growing over time in a hypercompetitive industry. To fix ideas assume that we are dealing with a specific industry such as personal computers and let y denote its sales or output and x_1, x_2 be the two inputs capital and labor subject to a Cobb-Douglas production function

$$Y = \beta_{0t} + \beta_1 X_1 + \beta_2 X_2 \tag{3}$$

where $Y = \ln y$ and $X_i = \ln x_i$, i=1,2.

Now consider a firm on the technical efficiency frontier. If the firm has resource efficiency (E_r), then the economies of scale in supply (i.e., $\beta_1 + \beta_2 > 1.0$) enjoyed by the incumbent make it difficult for a new entrant to offer competitive prices because the incumbent's higher volume reduces its costs. Other types of barriers around the stronghold enjoyed by the incumbent may include ownership of distribution channels with low cost supplies of inputs in the form of lower prices q_i for inputs x_i through overseas subsidiaries. These barriers provide an important source of competitive advantage because they allow the company to earn rents in protected markets. Finally, on taking the time derivative of equation (3) one can easily derive the growth equation

$$\dot{y}/y = \dot{\beta}_{0t}/\beta_{0t} + \beta_1 \dot{x}_1/x_1 + \beta_2 \dot{x}_2/x_2 \qquad (3.2)$$

Here the term $\dot{\beta}_{0t}/\beta_{0t}$ represents total factor productivity growth (TFP) or the Solow residual representing technological progress. Recently Hall (1990) developed a modified Solow residual by incorporating the presence of market power measured by the mark-up ratio μ and the increasing returns to scale index γ as follows:

$$\frac{\dot{\beta}_{0t}}{\beta_{0t}} = \frac{\dot{y}}{y} - \beta_1 \frac{\dot{x}_1}{x_1} - (1-\beta_1)\frac{\dot{x}_2}{x_2} - (\mu-1)\beta_1\left(\frac{\dot{x}_2}{x_2} - \frac{\dot{x}_1}{x_1}\right) - (\gamma-1)\dot{x}_1/x_1 \qquad (3.3)$$

Hall's statistical estimates found important empirical evidence for the existence of market power ($\mu > 1.0$) and also increasing returns to scale ($\gamma > 1.0$) in several sectors of the US economy. Clearly the innovations efficiency E_i would augment the value of γ much above unity and the access efficiency E_a and resource efficiency would substantially raise the value μ of mark-up above unity.

The capital input x_1 in the production function (3.1) needs an extended interpretation for capturing the dynamic implications of hypercompetition. This input must comprise both physical capital and human capital (H), where the learning and cumulative experience are important characteristics of H. In new growth theory Romer (1990) has used a production function involving the level of technology A, human capital allocated to the research sector H_A and physical capital $\hat{x}_1$, where H_A and H_y denote the two components of human capital allocated to research and output respectively

$$\begin{aligned} y &= f(H_y, A, \hat{x}_1, x_2) \\ &= \hat{x}_1^{\beta_1}(x_2 A)^{\beta_2}(H_y A)^{1-\beta_1-\beta_2} B^{\beta_1+\beta_2^{-1}} - 1 \end{aligned} \qquad (3.4)$$

where B is a productivity parameter in the optimal demand equation for $\hat{x}_1$. The research input in this model is the aggregate stock of designs, which is nothing but A in this formulation where A is assumed to grow according to the following path

$$\dot{A} = \phi H_A A \qquad (3.5)$$

where ϕ is a positive productivity parameter. Clearly the research sector in this model exhibits increasing returns to scale. Thus any innovations policy, which encourages research, has the effect of increasing the productivity of A through ϕH_A, which in turn favorably affects the growth of output.

Another formula due to Lucas (1993) emphasizes the externalities from a learning spillover technology. This spillover gives those who are operating near the production frontier a definite advantage in moving beyond it. Rivalry in hypercompetition only accentuates this by the successful firms rapidly increasing the dynamic resource efficiency E_r. Lucas used the production function in the following form

$$y = A x_1^{\beta_1} [u(t) H x_2]^{1-\beta_1} H_e^{\gamma} \qquad (3.6)$$
$$\dot{H}/H = \phi(1 - u(t))$$

Here H is the skill level of human capital with H_e denoting its learning spillover effect, x_1 is the physical capital and A is the technology level. Also u(t) is the proportion of labor time devoted to current production, so that $(1 - u(t))$ is the proportion devoted to human capital accumulation with ϕ as its productivity parameter. Thus there are no diminishing returns to the stock of human capital as in Romer's model.

Thus in the two input formulation (3.2) we have to interpret the input x_1 as the composite of both physical and human capital such that β_1 would tend to exceed one for a growing hypercompetitive firm and the technological progress term $\dot{\beta}_{0t}/\beta_{0t}$ should incorporate the learning spillover effect. In a static framework the optimal expansion path of a firm may be solved from a cost minimization model as follows:

$$\text{Min } C = q_1 x_1 + q_2 x_2$$
$$\text{s.t. } \sum_{j=1}^{N} X_{ij}\lambda_j \leq X_i; \sum_{j=1}^{N} Y_j \lambda_j \geq Y \qquad (4.1)$$
$$\sum_{j=1}^{N} \lambda_j = 1, \lambda_j \geq 0; j = 1, 2, ..., N$$

Here $X_{ij} = \ln x_{ij}$, $X_i = \ln x_i$, $Y_j = \ln y_j$ and $Y = \ln y$ and there are N firms in the industry, where the optimal inputs x_i are chosen given the input prices q_i.

The efficient firms must lie on the production frontier. Hence if firm j is on the production frontier then we must have

$$C_j = C^*; y_j = y^*, x_{ij} = x_j^*$$
$$Y_j^* = \ln y_j^* = \tilde{\beta}_0 + \sum_{i=1}^{z} \tilde{\beta}_i X_{ij} \qquad (4.2)$$
$$\tilde{\beta}_0 = \beta_0/a, \tilde{\beta}_i = \beta_i/a$$

where β_1, β_2, a and β_0 are the respective Lagrange multipliers for the constraint of model (4.1). Clearly if $Y_j < Y^*$ or $X_{ij} \neq X_i^*$ then the firm is not production efficient, since there exists a convex combination in the input output space, where the optimal output Y^* is higher than the observed Y_j, or the optimal input X_i^* is lower than X_{ij}.

The optimal expansion path may therefore be expressed as

$$x_2^* = v\, x_1^* \text{ where } v = (\beta_2 q_1)/(\beta_1 q_2) \qquad (4.3)$$

Assuming β_1, β_2 to be constant but varying input prices the output growth along the optimal expansion path may be easily derived for an efficient firm j as

$$\dot{y}_j^*/y_j^* = (\dot{\tilde{\beta}}_0^*/\tilde{\beta}_0^*) + \tilde{\beta}_2^*(\dot{v}/v) + (\tilde{\beta}_1^* + \tilde{\beta}_2^*)(\dot{x}_1^*/x_1^*) \qquad (4.4)$$

Note that the growth of capital inputs $\dot{x}_1^*/x_1^*$ must be viewed as a composite input comprising human capital and learning spillovers, i.e.,

$$\dot{x}_1^*/x_1^* = f(\dot{H}, \dot{A}/A)$$

If supply growth matches demand growth as $\dot{D}/D = kg$, then the optimal input growth for the efficient firms follows the balanced path

$$\dot{x}_1^*/x_1^* = \dot{x}_2^*/x_2^* = \left(\tilde{\beta}_1^* + \tilde{\beta}_2^*\right)^{-1} kg$$

if the coefficient β_0^* and v are constants. If returns to scale are constant and k = 1.0, i.e., no demand economies of scale, then the output (y*) and each optimal input (x_i^*) grow at the balanced rate of demand (g).

If the firms are not efficient in terms of the model (4.1) then their costs are higher than the optimal, i.e., $C_j > C^*$ and hence their prices are not competitive. Hence these firms are vulnerable to hypercompetition, i.e., their probability of exit is much higher as the positive gap ($C_j - C^*$) gets larger.

Now we consider the dynamics of the long run expansion path, where the efficient firm solves the following optimization model with two inputs: labor (x_2) and the composite capital (x_1):

$$\text{Min } C_T = \int_0^{T \to \infty} \exp(-\rho t)(q_1 x_1(t) + q_2 x_2(t)) dt$$

$$\text{s.t.} \quad y(t) = f(x_1, \dot{x}_1, x_2) \tag{5.1}$$

where $f(\cdot)$ is a log-linear Cobb-Douglas production function with increasing returns to scale. On applying Pontryagin's maximum principle the optimal trajectory for the two inputs may be explicitly computed as

$$\rho \, \theta f_3 - q_1(t) - \dot{\theta}(t) f_3 - \theta \dot{f}_3 = -\theta f_1$$
$$\theta f_2(t) = q_2(t); \theta = \theta(t) = \text{Lagrange multiplier} \tag{5.2}$$
$$\text{and } f_i = \partial f / \partial x_i \text{ where } x_3 = \dot{x}_1$$

In the steady state the first trajectory reduced to

$$q_1 = \theta f_1 \tag{5.3}$$

i.e., the value of marginal product of the composite capital input equals the input price. The same result holds in (5.2) if f_3 is zero, i.e., $\partial f / \partial \dot{x}_1 = 0$ or, investment is more productivity increasing. In the more general case when f_3 is positive but $\dot{f}_3$ is zero, i.e., constant marginal productivity of investment, then we obtain

$$f_3 = [\rho \theta + \dot{\theta}(t)]^{-1}(q_1(t) - \theta f_1)$$

This is the optimal condition linking the marginal productivities of the composite capital stock $x_1(t)$ and its rate of change $x_3(t)$. This is comparable to the so-called perfect foresight condition in optimal growth theory in macroeconomics; see, e.g., Sengupta (1998a, b). As in the static framework those firms not on the optimal cost frontier denoted by C_T^* would have higher costs and hence they would be vulnerable to competitive pressures to exit from the market. If there are N_1 efficient firms on the cost frontier they can be ranked in an escalation ladder from the highest to the lowest optimal costs.

Linear Model of Efficiency Growth

We consider now a linear DEA model for characterizing the dynamic efficiency frontier in terms of the growth of inputs and output. Assume the industry to be composed of N firms, where each firm j has m inputs x_{ij} and a single output y_j, such that the first m_1 inputs are current and the rest are capital inputs. The growth of inputs and outputs are denoted by $g_{ij} = \Delta x_{ij}/x_{ij}$ and $z_j = \Delta y_j/y_j$. Now one may formulate two different ways of specifying the growth efficiency frontier. One is to associate an imputed cost with respect to each $g_i = \Delta x_i/x_i$ and minimize the sum of such costs for all the inputs, both current and capital inputs. The second method computes a set of optimal weights for inputs and output in order to test for growth efficiency. The latter method of efficiency analysis is a modification of the recent techniques of data envelopment analysis (DEA), which has been discussed in some detail by Sengupta (2000a) in the context of growth frontier analysis.

In terms of the first approach one solves for the optimal input ($g_i = \Delta x_i/x_i$) and output growths ($z = \Delta y/y$) from the input output data of N firms as

$$\text{Min } \hat{C} = \sum_{i=1}^{m} \hat{q}_i g_i$$

$$\text{s.t.} \quad \sum_{j=1}^{N} g_{ij}\lambda_j \leq g_i \quad i = 1, 2, ..., m$$

$$\sum_{j=1}^{N} z_j \lambda_j \geq z \quad (6.1)$$

$$\Sigma \lambda_j = 1, \lambda_j \geq 0$$

Denoting optimal values by asterisks and the Lagrangean as

$$L = -\Sigma \hat{q}_i g_i + \sum_i \beta_i (g_i - \sum_{j=1}^{N} g_{ij}\lambda_j) + a(\sum_{j=1}^{N} z_j\lambda_j - z) + \beta_0(1 - \Sigma \lambda_j)$$

the optimal production frontier could be specified by the duality theorem as

$$z_j = (\beta_0^*/a^*) + \sum_{i=1}^{m} (\beta_i^*/a^*)g_{ij} \qquad (6.2)$$

where the Lagrange multiplier β_0^* is free in sign. If the firm j is not on the dynamic production frontier, then we have

$$z_j < \text{RHS of (6.2)} \qquad (6.3)$$

i.e., output growth is less than the optimal.

In the second case one solves for θ and ϕ to test the dynamic efficiency of firm k in terms of the following linear programming (LP) model:

$$\begin{aligned}
\text{Max } & \phi - \theta \\
\text{s.t. } & \sum_{j=1}^{N} g_{ij}\lambda_j \leq \theta g_{ik}; i = 1,2,...,m \\
& \sum_{j=1}^{N} z_j\lambda_j \geq \phi z_k \\
& \Sigma \lambda_j = 1, \lambda_j \geq 0; j = 1,2,...,N
\end{aligned} \qquad (6.4)$$

Firm k is dynamically efficient if $\theta^* = 1.0 = \phi^*$ and the equality holds in the constraints above. It is not efficient if $\theta^* < 1.0$, or $\phi^* > 1.0$ and the equality holds in the input and output constraints. This is so because it involves wastage of inputs, outputs or both. By duality the efficient firm j would follow the production frontier

$$z_j = (\beta_0^*/a^*) + \sum_{i=1}^{m} (\beta_i^*/a^*)g_{ij} \qquad (6.5)$$

where the Lagrangean function is

$$L = \phi - \theta + \sum_{i=1}^{m} \beta_i(\theta g_{ik} - \sum_{j=1}^{N} g_{ij}\lambda_j) + a(\Sigma z_j \lambda_j - \phi z_k) + \beta_0(1 - \Sigma \lambda_j)$$

Note that instead of one year growth rates one could use τ period average growth rates $g_{ij}(\tau)$, $z_j(\tau)$ in order to test which subset of N firms in the hypercompetitive industry satisfies dynamic or growth efficiency. Once this efficient subset is determined one could rank the efficient firms from the lowest to the highest growth rates.

The two subsets of dynamically efficient and inefficient firms in the industry determined by the linear models (6.1) and (6.4) above may by empirically used to test the intensity and impact of hypercompetition. Such an empirical application to the US personal computer industry has been made by Sengupta (2000a). This application evaluates the relative static and dynamic efficiency of 400 PC firms with an SIC code of 3570/3571 over a 5 year period 1984-1989. The data set is from Standard and Poor's Compustat Database and two variants of the linear model (6.4) of efficiency are computed. One tests the level efficiency of firms in terms of the input x_{ij} and output y_j, the other growth efficiency in terms of the growth inputs g_{ij} and growth output z_j. Two broad results of this study are: the growth efficient firms exhibit much faster output growth than the inefficient ones. Also the growth efficient firms reveal a much stronger showing in terms of overall growth than level efficiency.

Secondly, if output variance σ_y^2 is computed for the growth efficient firms (e.g., 12 in our application) in each year and also the mean $\bar{y}$, then this variance and mean are much higher for the efficient subset than the inefficient subset. Also the variance σ_y^2 is increasing over time thus implying volatility as is hypothesized in (1) before. Sengupta (2000b) has analyzed elsewhere other implications of access and innovations efficiency in this framework in some detail.

The companies included here comprise such well-known firms as Apple, Compaq, Dell, IBM, HP and also lesser-known firms such as AST Research, Toshiba, NBI, etc. Due to a variety of differentiated products, a composite output represented by total sales revenue is used as the single output for each company. Ten inputs are included comprising R&D expenses, net capital employed, plant and equipment and several marketing costs. The contribution of R&D efficiency for 12 efficient firms was 39%

and 13% for the 28 inefficient ones. Plant and equipment efficiency contributed 21% to growth efficiency for the efficient firms and 18% for the inefficient. The contribution of Solow-type technical progress was 35% for the efficient firms and only 12% for the rest. The output trends $\Delta y = a_0 + a_1 y(t)$ were as follows.

	a_0	a_1	a_2	R^2
Efficient firms $N_1 = 12$	-0.602	0.019*	-	0.961
Inefficient firms $N_2 = 28$	-	0.009*	-0.004	0.954

Here asterisk denotes significant t at 5% level and a_2 is the coefficient for a logistic trend: $\Delta y/y(t) = a_1 + a_2 y$. Clearly the growth efficient firms exhibit much faster growth than the inefficient firms. Clearly, a variety of growth patterns are possible in a hypercompetitive industry. For example the efficient sector may grow exponentially but the inefficient sector may follow a lower growth path or a logistic path. This is because the competitive vulnerability risk increases over time for the inefficient firms, when the efficiency gap between itself and the most efficient firm(s) in the industry increases.

4.2 Efficiency in Industry Equilibrium

One of the key premises of neoclassical economics is that market competition promotes economic efficiency. Free competition forces firms to reduce unit costs and the industry equilibrium ensures an optimal number of firms which meets total demand at minimal cost. This may be easily modeled in two stages. At the first stage each firm attempts to attain cost efficiency by striving to remain on the cost frontier. This stage compares the relative efficiency of different firms in terms of costs and selects only the efficient ones. At the second stage the industry selects the optimal number of firms, which minimizes total industry costs subject to the condition that supply equals or exceeds total demand.

Competition has been most intense in recent times in the new technology-based industries such as computers and telecommunications. Declining prices and average costs, accelerating global demand and increasing innovation efficiency have intensified the competitive pressure in these industries. The key role in this competitive pressure has been played by the cost efficiency of individual firms and the increasing market share of the cost efficient firms over time. At the industry level this has also intensified the potential exit rate (declining market share) of firms, which failed to remain on the leading edge of the cost efficiency frontier.

Our objective in this section is two-fold. One is to analyze the dynamics of the market selection process in this competitive environment, where cost efficient firms prosper and grow and the less efficient ones decline and fall. The second is to analyze the cost efficiency of a firm in a nonparametric way based only on the observed cost and output data of firms comprising the whole industry.

Our analysis follows a two-stage approach. In the first stage each firm minimizes costs, given the market price. The estimation of the firm's cost frontier is obtained through a nonparametric approach, which has been adopted in recent years. This nonparametric approach initially developed by Farrell (1957) and later generalized in the theory of data envelopment analysis (DEA), see e.g., Charnes et al. (1994) and Sengupta (2000) estimates the cost frontier of a firm by a convex hull method based on the observed cost and output data of all firms. Unlike the method of least squares it does not purport to estimate an *average* cost function, i.e., it attempts to estimate cost-specific (input specific) efficiency of each firm relative to all other firms in the industry.

In the second stage the market clearing price is determined in the industry by minimizing total industry costs. The dynamics of adjustment around the industry equilibrium is then analyzed by a Walrasian process, where prices rise in response to excess demand and fall in response to excess supply and the firm's output adjusts according to profitability.

In the DEA models of efficiency analysis the cost efficiency has been separately analyzed from market efficiency. Thus Athanassopoulos and Thanassoulis (1995), and also Norman and Stoker (1991) analyzed market efficiency in a two-stage approach, where the relative efficiency of an individual firm in capturing its share of the total market is analyzed by a linear programming (LP) version of the DEA model. We attempt here to generalize this method by explicitly allowing a semiparametric treatment of the first stage. In the first stage we estimate a cost frontier in a quadratic convex form for a firm. The second stage allows the market selection process to select the most efficient of the firms specified to be cost efficient in the first stage. This method is very similar to the economic approach of Farrell and Johansen (1972). Farrell applied the convex hull method of estimation of technical efficiency without using any market prices but mentioned allocative efficiency at the industry level, when the input and output prices are assumed to be determined by the demand supply equilibrium in the market. Johansen used the individual firm's production frontiers to determine the industry production frontier by maximizing total industry output under the constraints imposed by the aggregate inputs and the convex technology.

In our approach we consider first the problem of estimation of the firm-specific cost frontier. Let C_h and C_h^* be the cost function and the cost frontier (i.e., minimal cost function) of firm h, where $\varepsilon_h = C_h - C_h^* \geq 0$ indicates cost inefficiency. We assume C_h^* to be strictly convex and for simplicity to be quadratic, e.g., $C_h^* = \gamma_0 + \gamma_1 y_h + \gamma_2 y_h^2$, where y is output and the parameters γ_0, γ_1, γ_2 are all positive. For estimation of these parameters by the DEA approach we set up the LP model

$$\text{Min } \varepsilon_h = C_h - C_h^*$$
$$\text{s.t.} \quad C_j \geq \gamma_0 + \gamma_1 y_j + \gamma_2 y_j^2; j = 1, 2, \ldots, n \tag{7.1}$$

based on n observations (C_j, y_j). Here total costs C_j include both variable and fixed costs and all firms are assumed to follow a given common technology. Timmer (1971) applied a variant of this method by minimizing the sum of absolute values of errors $\sum_{h=1}^{n} |\varepsilon_h|$, since his interest was in *robust* estimation of the production function. Sengupta (1990) has discussed other forms of estimation including corrected ordinary least squares and the generalized method of moments. The main advantage of this type of DEA estimation is that it is firm specific. To see this more clearly one may consider the dual of the LP problem (7.1):

$$\text{Min } \sum_{j=1}^{n} \lambda_j C_j$$
$$\text{s.t.} \quad \sum_{j=1}^{n} \lambda_j y_j \geq y_h; \sum_{j=1}^{n} \lambda_j y_j^2 \geq y_h^2 \tag{7.2}$$
$$\sum_j \lambda_j = 1; \lambda_j \geq 0; j = 1, 2, \ldots, n$$

This can also be written as

$$\text{Min } \theta \quad \text{s.t.} \quad \lambda \in R$$

and

$$R = \left\{ \sum_{j=1}^{n} \lambda_j C_j \leq \theta C_h \text{ and the constraints of (7.2)} \right\} \quad (7.3)$$

and λ is the column vector with n elements (λ_j) representing nonnegative weights of the convex combination of costs for each firm. Here θ is a scalar representing a measure of inefficiency, i.e., $\theta^* = 1.0$ indicates 100% efficiency and $\theta^* < 1.0$ denotes less than full efficiency, i.e., relative inefficiency.

On using the Lagrangean function

$$L = -\theta + \beta(\theta C_h - \Sigma \lambda_j C_j) + \alpha_1 (\Sigma \lambda_j y_j - y_h) + \alpha_2 (\Sigma \lambda_j y_j^2 - y_h^2) + \beta_0$$

and applying Kuhn-Tucker conditions one obtains the cost frontier for firm j, when all the slack variables are zero

$$C_j = \gamma_0 + \gamma_1 y_j + \gamma_2 y_j^2; \gamma_i \geq 0; i = 0,1,2 \quad (7.4)$$

where

$$\gamma_0 = \beta_0 / \beta, \gamma_1 = \alpha_1 / \beta \text{ and } \gamma_2 = \alpha_2 / \beta$$

On varying h in the index set $I_n = \{1,2,\ldots,n\}$ the cost efficiency frontier for all the firms can be determined. Note that for any firm h which is less than 100% efficient, i.e., $\theta^* < 1.0$, one can adjust its cost C_j to $\theta^* C_j$ so that in terms of the adjusted cost firm h will be 100% efficient. In this case the cost frontier for firm h can be written as

$$C_h = \tilde{\gamma}_0 + \tilde{\gamma}_1 y_j + \tilde{\gamma}_2 y_h^2 \quad (7.5)$$

where $\tilde{\gamma}_i = \gamma_i / \theta^*$, i=0,1,2. Thus the set of all cost efficient frontiers can be specified. The second stage of the market demand process selects among this set, so that the total industry cost (TC) is minimized. But since the cost frontiers of firms are not all identical, we have to assume that firms are identified by their cost structures, where each firm is assumed to belong to one of m possible types of costs, each producing a homogenous output. Let n_j be the number of firms of type $j=1,2,\ldots,m$ cost structure. We now minimize TC for the whole industry, i.e.,

$$\underset{\{n_j,y_j\}}{\text{Min }} TC = \sum_{j=1}^{m} n_j C_j(y_j)$$

$$\text{s.t.} \quad \sum_{j=1}^{m} n_j y_j \geq D; (n_j, y_j) \geq 0 \tag{7.6}$$

where $C_j = C_j(y_j)$ denotes the cost frontier of firm j in terms of either (7.4) or (7.5). Total market demand D is assumed to be given. Clearly if $D > 0$, then we must have $n_j y_j > 0$ for some $j=1,2,\ldots,m$. On using p as the Lagrange multiplier for the market demand supply constraint and assuming the vector $n = (n_1, n_2, \ldots, n_m)$ to be given, total industry cost TC in (7.6) is minimized if and only if the following conditions hold for given $D > 0$,

$$MC_j(y_j) - p(n,D) \geq 0 \tag{7.7}$$

and

$$y_j[MC_j(y_j) - p(n,D)] = 0, \text{ for all j}$$

where $MC_j = MC_j(y_j)$ is the marginal cost frontier, i..., $MC_j = \lambda_1 + 2\lambda_2 y_h$ and $p = p(n,D)$ may be interpreted as the market clearing price, i.e., the shadow price which equates total supply $S = \Sigma n_j y_j$ to demand D. Let $\hat{y}_j = \hat{y}_j(p)$ be the optimal solution to (7.6). Then clearly it follows that $\hat{y}_j$ variables are continuous functions of D and vector n. Optimal total costs can then be specified as

$$TC = \sum_{j=1}^{m} n_j C_j(\hat{y}_j(n,D)) \tag{7.8}$$

Clearly TC(n) here is a convex function, hence its minimum exists. Let TC(n) reach its minimum at $\hat{n}$. Then $TC(n) \geq TC(\hat{n})$ for all $n \geq 0$. By Kuhn-Tucker conditions it holds that $\hat{n} = (\hat{n}_j)$ satisfies the following

$$p = AC_j(\hat{y}_j); \hat{y}_j > 0$$
$$p = MC_j(\hat{y}_j); \hat{y}_j > 0 \tag{7.9}$$

where $AC_j(\hat{y}_j)$ is average cost at the optimal output vector $\hat{y} = (\hat{y}_j)$. Thus the long run equilibrium price p is at the minimum point of the $AC_j(\hat{y}_j)$ curve, i.e., the minimum efficient scale (MSE) is attained at this price. At this equilibrium price firm j has its capacity fully utilized.

Several economic implications of this result may now be discussed. First of all, if the market demand function is viewed in its inverse form, i.e., $p = F(D)$ where $D = \hat{Y}$, $\hat{Y}$ being the aggregate output, then

$$F(Y) \geq LRAC(\hat{y}) \text{ as } Y \leq \hat{Y}$$

where LR denotes the long run. But since $LRAC(y_j)$ is of the form

$$LRAC(y_j) = \frac{\gamma_0}{y_j} + \gamma_1 + \gamma_2 y_j$$

its minimum is attained at

$$\hat{y}_j = (\gamma_0/\gamma_2)^{1/2} = (\gamma_{0j}/\gamma_{2j})^{1/2}$$
$$LRAC_j(\hat{y}_j) = \alpha_1 + 2\sqrt{\gamma_0 \gamma_2}$$

Thus a dynamic process of entry (or increase in market share) or exit (or decrease in market share) can be specified as a Walrasian adjustment process

$$dn_j/dt = k_j(p - LRAC(\hat{y}_j))$$

and

$$dp/dt = b(D(p) - (\hat{Y})) \qquad (7.10)$$

where k_j and b are positive parameters. The equilibrium is then given by the steady state values $p^* = LRAC(\hat{y})$ and $D(p^*) = (\hat{Y})$. This entry (exit) rule (7.10) is different from the limit pricing rule developed by Gaskins (1971) and others, in that this is determined directly from the estimate of MES of cost efficient firms. Also different cost structures are allowed here, which implies that in terms of minimum average costs different firms can be ranked. For example if firms are ordered from the lowest to highest according to minimum average costs $\hat{c}_j$ as follows:

$$\hat{c}_{(1)} < \hat{c}_{(2)} < ... < \hat{c}_{(k)}, k \leq n$$

then $p_{(1)} = \hat{c}_{(1)}$ would be the lowest price, whereas $p_{(k)} = \hat{c}_{(k)}$ would be the highest. Hence if due to exogenous demand shift the price p comes down to $p = p_{(1)}$, then all other firms have to exit in the long run. Likewise if demand shift raises the price to $p = p_{(k)}$ then the other firms would earn positive *'rents'* as

$$\Delta_{(j)} = p_{(j)} - p_{(1)}, j = 2, 3, ..., k \tag{7.11}$$

Low cost firms can produce at a lower AC than the others, because they may possess some scarce factor, such as superior technology, which is not available to others. Thus the low cost firms may earn for some time more than normal profits, i.e., excess profits. Some potential entrants, seeing the large profits made by the low cost firms, would want to adopt the superior technology, thus wiping out the extra rent. Until this happens, the low-cost firms would enjoy positive differential rent, i.e., early adopter's profit advantage. Thus in the long run the variance of $\hat{c}_{(j)}$ or of differential rent $\Delta_{(j)}$ would decline, though it may be high in the short run.

Now consider the case when each firm j has a similar cost function $C_j(y_j)$, i.e., m=1. The industry model then takes a simple form

$$\text{Min } \sum_{j=1}^{n} C_j(y_j)$$
$$\text{s.t. } \Sigma y_j \geq D; y_j \geq 0; j \in I_n \tag{7.12}$$

By rewriting the cost function as $C_j(y_j; k_j)$ where k_j is the capital endowment, short and long run cases can be distinguished. The short run case assumes k_j to be constant so that the cost function depends on output only while in the long run case the cost function depends on output and capital inputs, which are both variable. In the long run case the Lagrangean function can be written as

$$L = -\sum_{j=1}^{n} C_j(y_j, k_j) + p(\Sigma y_j - D)$$

$$= \sum_{j=1}^{n} \left[py_j - C_j(y_j, k_j)\right] - pD \qquad (7.13)$$

$$= \sum_{j=1}^{n} \pi_j - pD$$

where π_j is the profit function of firm j, if p is interpreted as the market clearing price. In a competitive industry each firm is a price taker, so the market price is given as $\hat{p}$. In the short run the capital inputs are also given as $\hat{k}_j$. Hence the vector $Y^* = (y_1^*, y_2^*, ..., y_n^*)$ is a short run industry equilibrium (SRIE) if each firm j maximizes profit π_j with respect to y_j. Since the profit function is strictly concave, this SRIE $Y^*(\hat{K})$ exists and it is unique for every given vector $\hat{K} = (\hat{k}_1, \hat{k}_2, ..., \hat{k}_n)$. For the long run industry equilibrium LRIE we have to modify the objective function as long run profits defined as

$$W_j = \int_0^{\infty} e^{-\rho t} [\pi_j(t) - h(u_j(t)] dt \qquad (7.14)$$

where u(t) is investment defined by $dk_j/dt = u_j(t) - \delta_j k_j(t)$, $h(u_j(t))$ is a convex cost function and δ is the fixed rate of depreciation.

The LRIE is now defined by vectors K*, Y* if for each firm j,

(i) y_j^* maximizes W_j for given k_j,

(ii) k_j^* maximizes W_j for given y_j^* \qquad (7.15)

But since the investment cost function is separable, the maximization problem (i) is equivalent to max π_j.

Here $\hat{p} = p(\hat{y}) = p(y^*)$ and $\hat{y} = y^* = \sum_{j=1}^{n} \hat{y}_j$. Thus the industry equilibrium price p* clears the market and given p* each firm maximizes long run profit with respect to y_j and k_j. Now define a *competitive industry* *equilibrium* by vectors Y*, K* and price p* such that $D = D(p^*) = \Sigma\, y_j^*$ and the conditions (7.15) hold. Then one can easily prove that such competitive industry equilibrium exists, since the cost functions are strictly convex and the profit function strictly concave; see e.g., Dreze and Sheshinski (1984).

Dynamic Adjustments

Two types of dynamic adjustments are implicit in the two-stage model of competitive industry equilibrium outlined in earlier sections. One is the path of optimal accumulation of capital by each efficient firm j, which maximizes the discounted stream of profits. This involves a continuous adjustment of existing capacity (capital) by an optimal investment program so as to reduce the current cost of using existing capacity for producing current outputs. For example, consider a quadratic cost function $h_j = g_1 u_j + g_2 u_j^2$ for each firm j, which solves the dynamic problem

$$\underset{u_j}{\text{Min}} \int_0^\infty e^{-\rho t}\left[\gamma_0 + \gamma_1 y_j + \gamma_2 y_j^2 + \beta_1 k_j + \beta_2 k_j^2 + h_j\right] dt$$

$$\text{s.t.} \quad \dot{k}_j = u_j - \delta k_j;\ \dot{k}_j = dk_j/dt$$

$$k_j(0) > 0 \text{ given}$$

On using the current value Hamiltonian involving k_j and u_j:

$$H = -\beta_1 k_j - \beta_2 k_j^2 - g_1 u_j - g_2 u_j^2 + \mu(u_j - \delta k_j)$$

Pontryagin's maximum principle yields the optimality conditions

$$\dot{\mu} = (\rho + \delta)\mu + \beta_1 + 2\beta_2 k_j$$

$$u_j = (2g_2)^{-1}(\mu - g_1)$$

$$\dot{k}_j = u_j - \delta k_j$$

On eliminating μ one obtains the pair of differential equations

$$\begin{pmatrix} \dot{u}_j \\ \dot{k}_j \end{pmatrix} = \begin{bmatrix} (\rho+\delta) & \beta_2/g_2 \\ 1 & -\delta \end{bmatrix} \begin{pmatrix} u_j \\ k_j \end{pmatrix} + \begin{pmatrix} A_1 \\ 0 \end{pmatrix} \quad (7.16)$$

where $A_1 = (\beta_1 + (\rho+\delta)g_1)/(2g_2)$

The characteristic equation is

$$\lambda^2 - \rho\lambda - [\delta(\rho+\delta) + \beta_2/g_2] = 0 \tag{7.17}$$

Since the product of two roots is negative and term

$$\rho^2 + 4\beta_2/g_2 + 4\delta(\rho+\delta)$$

is positive, the two roots are real, one positive and one negative. Hence there exists a saddle point equilibrium. The steady state levels are given by

$$\bar{k}_j = -(\beta_1 + g_1(\rho+\delta))/(\beta_2 + 2(\rho+\delta)\delta g_2)$$
$$\bar{u}_j = \delta\bar{k}_j$$

It is clear that as the cost coefficients g_1 or β_1 raise the steady state levels of capital and hence investments decline. The two characteristic roots imply that there is a stable manifold along which the motion of the system (7.16) is purely towards $(\bar{u}_j, \bar{k}_j)$ and an unstable manifold along which motion is exclusively away from $(\bar{u}_j, \bar{k}_j)$. By transversality conditions one may choose only the stable manifold. By using this stable manifold around the steady state equilibrium one may state the following proposition.

Proposition 1. For each vector K there exists a SRIE Y*(K), where each y_j^* maximizes $\pi_j = p^* y_j - C_j(y_j, k_j)$. There also exist a LRIE given by the pair (Y*, K*) where for each firm j:

(i) y_j^* solves $\max \pi_j \ p^* y_j - C_j(y_j, k_j^*)$

and

(ii) k_j^* and u_j^* solve the steady state level of profits

$$\bar{\pi}_j = p^* y_j^* - C_j(y_j^*, k_j) - h(u_j)$$

The SRIE and LRIE solutions are unique.

Proof: Existence follows from the fact that the production set is convex, closed and bounded by assumption. Strict concavity of the profit function yields uniqueness. Equilibrium market price $p^* = P(y^*)$, $y^* = \sum_{j=1}^{n} y_j^*$ equalizes total demand and supply.

The adjustment of the market equilibrium may be directly shown in terms of the Walrasian process of price quantity adjustments as specified in (7.10) before, e.g.,

$$\dot{y} = a[p - c(y)] \qquad (7.18)$$
$$\dot{p} = b[D(p) - y]$$

where c(y) is the long run minimal average cost function and a, b are positive parameters. The conditions for convergence to the steady state of this system are once again specified by its characteristic roots. Two important cases are:

(i) each root has a negative real part; this implies that the steady state equilibrium is globally stable, and

(ii) two real roots, one positive and one negative; this implies a saddle point equilibrium.

There is a stable manifold of convergence. Hence one can state the result.

Proposition 2. There exists a stable manifold along which the LRIE can be reached by a Walrasian adjustment process.

Proof: By using the explicit cost function assumed to be strictly convex, the two roots of the characteristic equation can be directly computed, e.g.,

$$\lambda^2 + (ac' - bD')\lambda + ab(1 - c'D') = 0 \qquad (7.19)$$

where $c' = \partial c / \partial y$, $D' = \partial D / \partial p$. Equation (7.19) has roots with negative real parts if and only if $ac' - bD' > 0$ and $(1 - c'D) > 0$. But with $D'(p) < 0, c' > 0$ implies that these conditions hold. In the second case if it holds that $c' < 1/D' < 0$, then one real root is positive and the other negative. Hence there exists a stable manifold of convergence.

Some important implications of the two dynamic adjustment processes have to be briefly mentioned. First of all, if individual firms do not follow these optimal paths of capital accumulation, then they would not be consistent with long run industry equilibrium. Also, firms, which are cost efficient in the short run, may not be so in the long run unless they use an optimal investment path. Hence there is scope for analyzing inefficiency in the long run. This aspect has been analyzed in a nonparametric framework by Sengupta (1999). Secondly, the competitive industry model developed here has a decentralization interpretation in terms of firms surviving under long run equilibrium; see e.g., Gabszewicz and Michel (1991). Novshek (1980) has shown that this type of equilibrium can be extended to include the case of Cournot equilibrium, if firm size is measured by technology, market size measured by perfectly competitive demand and if firms are small relative to the overall market and free entry conditions prevail. In such a case Cournot equilibrium exists and the aggregate output is approximately competitive. Finally, one could empirically test the consistency of the cost efficiency model (7.4) estimated by the DEA model in respect of the industry equilibrium. So long as MES levels are different for cost efficient firms, there exists some scope for improving efficiency in the long run. This implies price changes due to entry and exit of firm in the industry with a consequent impact on individual firms through allocative efficiency.

Allocative Efficiency Under Equilibrium

The industry equilibrium in competitive markets may be analyzed more directly if we assume that market clearing prices are estimated by a demand function $\hat{p} = a - by$, $y = \sum_{j=1}^{n} y_j$. In this case the industry equilibrium is directly obtained from maximizing total industry profits π, where the cost function of each firm is strictly convex and quadratic:

$$\underset{y_j}{\text{Max}}\, \pi = \Sigma[\hat{p}y_j - C_j(y_j)] \tag{7.20}$$

Since $\hat{p}$ is the market-clearing price, equilibrium of market demand and supply is implicit here. The industry selection process (7.20) selects optimal outputs y_j^* and $y^* = \Sigma y_j^*$ so as to meet total demand by following the rule

$$y_j^* = A_j - B_j y^* \tag{7.21}$$
$$y^* = (1 + \sum_j B_j)^{-1}(\Sigma A_j)$$

where $A_j = (b + 2\gamma_{2j})^{-1}(a - \gamma_{1j})$, $B_j = (b + 2\gamma_{2j})^{-1}b$.

Let c_j^* be the optimal average cost $C_j(y_j^*)/y_j^*$, then the entry or increased market share rule can be specified as

$$\dot{y}_j = k_j(\hat{p} - c_j^*), k_j > 0$$

i.e., entry (market share) is positive (increasing) or negative (decreasing) according as $\hat{p}$ exceeds (falls short of) c_j^*. The price adjustment in the market can be similarly specified as

$$\dot{p} = k(D(\hat{p}) - y^*), k > 0$$

The equilibrium supply behavior specified in (7.21) implies the following comparative static consequences:

$$\partial y_j^* / \partial \gamma_{2j} < 0, \partial y_j^* / \partial \gamma_{1j} < 0, \partial y_j^* / \partial b < 0$$

and $\partial y_j^* / \partial a > 0$

If all cost functions are identical so that $A_j = A$ and $B_j = B$ for all j, then one obtains

$$y_j^* = A - B(1 + nB)^{-1}(nA)$$
$$y_j^* = (1 + nB)^{-1}(nA); p = a - by^*$$

This shows the impact of the number of numbers in the industry on equilibrium industry output.

When firms are not alike in their cost functions but belong to a cost structure, each firm may follow one of m possible types of cost. Let n_j be the number of firms of type j=1,2,…,m cost structure. Then the allocative efficiency model (7.20) takes the form

$$\underset{n_j, y_j}{\text{Max } \pi} = \sum_{j=1}^{m} \hat{p} n_j y_j - \sum_{j=1}^{m} n_j C_j(y_j)$$

where $\hat{p} = a - b \sum_j n_j y_j$; $a, b > 0$. This yields the equilibrium conditions

$$p_j^* = \hat{p}(y_j^*) = \left(1 - \frac{1}{|\varepsilon_p|}\right)^{-1} MC_j(y_j^*)$$

$$p_j^* = AC_j(y_j^*)\left(1 - |\varepsilon_{n_j}|\right)^{-1}$$

where ε_p and ε_{n_j} are the price elasticity of demand and size elasticity of price respectively, i.e.,

$$\varepsilon_{n_j} = (\partial p/p)/(\partial n_j / n_j), \varepsilon_p = (\partial y_j / y_j)/(\partial p/p)$$

When $|\varepsilon_p|$ tends to infinity and e_{n_j} tends to zero then we obtain the earlier result (7.9), i.e.,

$$p = MC_j(y_j^*) = AC_j(y_j^*), y_j^* > 0$$

Thus we can state the result.

Proposition 3. There exists an industry equilibrium specified by the pair of vectors (n*, Y*), where n* = $(n_1, n_2, \ldots, n_m)$ and Y* = $(y_1^*, y_2^*, \ldots, y_n^*)$ which satisfy the optimality conditions (7.22). If each cost function is strictly convex and quadratic, then this equilibrium pair (n*, Y*) is unique. Furthermore, there exists a stable manifold along which the equilibrium could be reached from a nearby nonequilibrium point.

Proof: Since the profit function is closed and bounded by its continuity with respect to (n, Y) the existence of industry equilibrium is assured. By strict concavity the equilibrium is unique. Furthermore, the Walrasian adjustment process defined by the free entry (exit) rules possesses a stable manifold due to the negative slope of the demand function and strict convexity of the cost function.

Several implications of this proposition are important in economic terms. First of all, optimality of the industry equilibrium (n*, Y*) may be tested against the observed outputs y_j and firm sizes n_j. In cases of disequilibrium the observed values would differ from the optimum and hence the market process of adjustment through entry and exit has to be analyzed. Secondly, the impact of demand on equilibrium output and price can be directly evaluated in this framework. In particular, large demand fluctuations would tend to have some adverse reaction for the risk averse producers, e.g., their optimal output would tend to be lower. Finally, market concentration measured by unequal firm sizes would affect the industry equilibrium, e.g., firms with the least optimal average cost would survive longer.

Illustrative Application

In order to indicate the usefulness of the cost efficiency concepts developed here, we may illustrate their application in the US computer industry. Growth and efficiency in this industry over the period 1985-2000 have been analyzed by Sengupta (2002) in some detail elsewhere. Here we select 10 out of 22 companies from the earlier study and estimate minimum efficient scale (MES) for three selected years 1987, 1990 and 1997. The data set is taken from Standard and Poor's Compustat file. The total costs here comprise the following: R&D expense, cost of goods sold and the cost of plant and equipment net of depreciation. Cost of goods sold includes manufacturing, marketing and administrative costs and the cost of change in inventory. Total combined costs comprise 75 to 80% of overall costs. For the output measure 'net sales' data are used and these are not deflated due to lack of a suitable price index.

Since the cost components are not deflated and it is difficult to separate the short run and the long run components of total costs we adopt a nonradial measure of cost efficiency. This measure differs from a radial measure in that different components may grow or decline at different proportions. Thus in order to test the cost efficiency of firm h the following LP model is set up

$$\text{Min} \sum_{i=1}^{3} \theta_i$$

$$\text{s.t.} \quad \sum_{j=1}^{n} C_{ij}\lambda_j \leq \theta_i C_{ih}; i = 1,2,3 \tag{7.23}$$

$$\sum_{j=1}^{n} y_j\lambda_j \geq y_h; \Sigma y_j^2 \lambda_j \geq y_h^2$$

$$\Sigma \lambda_j = 1, \lambda_j \geq 0, j=1,2,\ldots,n$$

By using $C_j = \sum_{i=1}^{3} \beta_i C_{ij}$ as the total cost measure, where β_i's are the shadow prices of the first three constraints (7.23), one could derive the cost frontier specified by (7.4) before. The estimates of AC_j and min AC_j are then obtained and denoted by c_j and c_j^* and the gap $\varepsilon_j = c_j - c_j^*$ measures the scope of unutilized capacity.

Table 1 shows the estimates of c_j and ε_j for 10 selected companies and their rank in terms of closeness of ε_j to zero. These estimates are only illustrative, since the size is sometimes very small. Nevertheless, two broad results are indicated. First, there is a wide diversity in the pattern of average costs along the cost frontier; hence the levels of MES vary significantly. Thus Apple Computer seems to have the best cost structure at the end of 1980s and the beginning of 1990 but after 1995 the company had trouble in its marketing policy and its effects are evident in the ranking. By contrast Dell Computer retained its market share due to competitive pricing based on MES. Secondly, some firms like Maxwell and Encore did not perform very well from the beginning relative to the others and their market shares declined considerably. In the long run their survival is in great doubt. The R&D expenditure played a very critical role in maintaining the rank of a firm in the efficiency scale over time. The detailed implications of the role of R&D expenditure in growth and efficiency of US computer industry are discussed in Chapter 5.

Table 1. DEA Estimates of Average Cost (c_j) on the Frontier and its Minimal Value (c_j^*)

	1987			1990			1997		
Company	c_j	ε_j	rank	c_j	ε_j	rank	c_j	ε_j	rank
Apple	0.58	0.0	1	0.59	0.0	1	0.98	0.34	7
Compaq	0.76	0.18	3	0.83	0.25	6	0.82	0.18	5
Datapoint	0.86	0.28	6	0.69	0.11	3	0.76	0.12	3
Dell	0.74	0.16	2	0.73	0.15	4	0.81	0.17	4
HP	0.82	0.24	5	0.84	0.25	7	0.84	0.21	6
Hitachi	0.98	0.40	7	0.96	0.38	8	1.00	0.41	8
SGI	4	0.56	8	0.63	0.05	2	0.73	0.09	2
Sun	0.78	0.28	4	0.76	0.18	5	0.65	0.01	1
Maxwell	0.85	0.58	9	0.81	0.39	9	0.80	0.43	9
Encore	0.90	0.61	10	0.91	0.41	10	0.93	0.44	10
Optimal AC (average)	0.59			0.58			0.64		

References

- D'Aveni, R.A. (1994): Hypercompetition: Managing the Dynamics of Strategic Maneuvering. Free Press, New York
- Ebeling, W. (1991): Mutations and Selections in Evolutionary Processes, in Complexity, Chaos and Biological Evolution (P. Mosekilde and L. Mosekilde, eds.). Plenum Press, New York
- Fisher, R.A. (1930): The Genetical Theory of Natural Selection. Clarendon Press, Oxford
- Gaskins, D.W. (1971): Dynamic Limit Pricing: Optimal Pricing Under Threat of Entry. Journal of Economic Theory 3, 306-322
- Ginzberg, L.R. (1983): Theory of Natural Selection and Population Growth. Benjamin Cummings Publishing, Menlo Park, CA
- Hall, R.E. (1990): Invariance Properties of Solow's Productivity Residual, in P. Diamond (ed.), Growth, Productivity and Unemployment. MIT Press, Massachusetts
- Jovanovic, B. (1997): Learning and Growth, in D.M. Kreps and K. Wallis (eds.), Advances in Economics and Econometrics: Theory and Applications. Cambridge University Press, New York
- Lucas, R.E. (1993): Making a Miracle. Econometrica 61, 251-272
- Metcalfe, J.S. (1994): Competition, Evolution and the Capital Market. Metroeconomica 45, 127-154
- Milgrom, P., Roberts, J. (1982): Limit Pricing and Entry Under Incomplete Information: An Equilibrium Analysis. Econometrica 50, 443-459
- Porter, M.E. (1987): From Competitive Advantage to Corporate Strategy. Harvard Business Review 65, 43-59
- Romer, P.M. (1990): Are Nonconvexities Important for Understanding Growth. American economic Review 80, 97-103
- Sengupta, J.K. (1998b): Stochastic Learning by Doing in New Growth Theory. Keio Economic Studies 35(2), 9035
- Sengupta, J.K. (1998a): New Growth Theory: An Applied Perspective. Edward Elgar, Cheltenham, UK
- Sengupta, J.K. (2000a): Dynamic and Stochastic Efficiency Analysis: Economics of Data Envelopment Analysis. World Scientific, London
- Sengupta, J.K. (2000b): Efficiency Under Hypercompetition in the Computer Industry. Unpublished paper
- Shapiro, C., Varian, H.L. (1999): Information Rules: A Strategic Guide to the Network Economy. Harvard Business School Press, Cambridge, Massachusetts

- Thomas, L.G. (1998): The Two Faces of Competition, in Ilinitch, A., Lewin, A. and D'Aveni, R. (eds.), Managing in Times of Disorder. Sage Publication, Thousand Oaks, CA

5
Growth and Efficiency in Computer Industry

Competition and technological change has been most rapid in the computer industry today and its impact on cost efficiency and productivity growth has been most significant for the US economy over the last two decades. Thus Norsworthy and Jang (1992) have empirically found for the US computer industry a productivity growth rate of 2 percent per year for the period 1958-96, while for the recent period 1992-98 the growth exceeded 2.5 percent per year on the average. Increased R&D investment and expanding 'knowledge capital' have contributed significantly to this productivity growth. They helped reduce marginal costs and prices, which led to increases in overall demand. Thus according to the recent estimate by Jorgenson and Stiroh (2000) the price decline for personal computes has accelerated in recent years reaching nearly 28 percent per year from 1995 to 1998. Significant economies of scale and learning curve effects have often been the key to this rapid price decline.

Our object in this chapter is to analyze the sources of growth and efficiency in US computer industry over the period (1985-2000) in terms of a production frontier approach. Unlike the time series estimates by regression, we consider here firm-specific measures of efficiency in a nonparametric way. The nonparametric approach focuses on output growth due to growth in inputs and technological progress and uses the observed data on changes in inputs and output in a convex hull method of characterizing a production frontier.

Modeling the efficiency measurement in a nonparametric way was first introduced by Farrell (1957) and later generalized to multiple outputs by the method known as data envelopment analysis in management science literature, see e.g., Charnes, Cooper et al. (1994) and Sengupta (2000). This method has found widespread applications in public sector organizations such as public schools and also private commercial enterprises such as banks.

We consider production frontier models for the firms in computer industry using a Cobb-Douglas specification. With one output (y_j) and m inputs (x_{ij}) for each firm j (j=1,2,...,N) we write the production function as

$$\ln y_j(t) = \beta_0 + \sum_{i=1}^{m} \beta_i \ln x_{ij}(t) + \varepsilon_j(t) \tag{1}$$

The time series data of inputs and output for the firms in US computer industry (1987-2000) exhibit nonstationarity in the random error term $\varepsilon_j(t)$. Hence the usual least squares estimate of production (1) is not valid, since the t and F tests no longer hold. However the input output data exhibit first difference stationarity, so that the transformed model

$$\Delta y_j(t)/y_j(t) = \Delta\beta_0 + \sum_i \beta_i(\Delta x_{ij}(t)/x_{ij}(t)) + \Delta\varepsilon_j(t)$$

has a stationary error structure, where least squares estimates are valid. We use this formulation in a nonparametric framework when we observe the vectors of output $\tilde{y}(t) = (\Delta y_j(t)/y_j(t))$ and inputs $\tilde{x}_j(t) = \Delta x_{ij}(t)/x_{ij}(t)$ for each t. Three types of nonparametric formulations will be used here. One formulation tests if firm h is relatively efficient in respect of other firms in the industry by solving the following linear programming (LP) model

$$\text{Min } J = \beta_0 + \beta'\tilde{x}_h(t)$$
$$\text{s.t. } \beta_0 + \beta'\tilde{x}_h(t) \geq \tilde{y}_j(t); j = 1, 2, ..., N \qquad (2)$$
$$\beta = (\beta_i) \geq 0; \beta_0 \text{ free in sign}$$

Here prime denotes transpose and β denotes the parameters β_i representing the coefficients of production of different inputs. Denoting optimal values by asterisk, firm h is observed to be growth efficient if it holds that

$$\beta_0^* + \beta^{*'}\tilde{x}_h(t) = \tilde{y}_h(t)$$

Otherwise it is not efficient, when its observed output growth $\tilde{y}_h(t)$ is less than its potential denoted by $\beta_0^*(t) + \beta^{*'}\tilde{x}_h(t)$.

If we impose a constraint on the parameters as

$$\sum_{i=1}^{m} \beta_i = 1 \qquad (3)$$

then we are assuming constant returns to scale (CRS). The nonparametric model (2) however exhibits variable returns to scale (VRS) since it does not impose the condition (3). Solow (1957) estimated an aggregate Cobb-Douglas production function for the US economy over the period 1909-1949 under the CRS assumption (3) and used a measure of technological progress (regress) as

$$\Delta A(t)/A(t) = \hat{\beta}_0$$

where $y(t) = A\Pi_i x_i^{\beta_i}$. Clearly this scale-constrained measure differs from the unconstrained measure obtained as β_0^* from the LP model (2) which exhibits VRS.

A second variant of the nonparametric approach sets up an input-oriented LP model to test for growth efficiency of a firm h. The LP model is of the form

$$\text{Min } \theta(t)$$

$$\text{s.t. } \sum_{j=1}^{N} \tilde{x}_j(t)\lambda_j(t) \leq \theta(t)\tilde{x}_h(t)$$

$$\sum_{j=1}^{N} \tilde{y}_j(t)\lambda_j(t) \geq \tilde{y}_h(t) \qquad (5)$$

$$\sum_{j=1}^{N} \lambda_j(t) = 1; \lambda_j \geq 0; j = 1, 2, ..., N; t = 1, 2, ..., T$$

Let $(\lambda^*(t), \theta^*(t))$ be the optimal solutions of (5). Then firm h is on the dynamic production efficiency frontier if $\theta^*(t) = 1$ and all the slacks are zero. If however $\theta^*(t)$ is positive but less than unity, then it is not dynamically production efficient, since it uses excess inputs measured by $(1-\theta^*(t))\tilde{x}_h(t)$. Thus, in case of production inefficiency of firm h, the input constraints in (5) show that a linear convex combination of other firms in the industry does better in using fewer inputs. Here $\theta^*(t)$ provides a radial measure of dynamic production efficiency at each t in terms of proportionate reduction of inputs. A more general measure would replace $\theta(t)$ by $\theta_i(t)$ for each input i and change the objective function as

$$\text{Min } \sum_{i=1}^{m} \theta_i(t) \qquad (6)$$

with $0 \leq \theta_i(t) \leq 1$. This measure is closely related to the measure developed by Russell (1985), Athanassopoulos (1997) and more recently by Ruggiero and Bretschneider (1998) who considered a weighted average Russell measure as $\Sigma\, w_i\theta_i(t)$. This nonradial measure quantifies the maximum average relative improvements (i.e., input reductions measured in percentages of the current levels) in the use of input usage.

Some implications of the dynamic efficiency model (5) may be noted. First of all, one may easily derive from the Lagrangean function

$$L = -\theta(t) + b'[\theta(t)\tilde{x}_h(t) - \sum_j \tilde{x}_j(t)\lambda_j(t)]$$
$$+ a[\sum_j \tilde{y}_h(t)\lambda_j(t) - \tilde{y}_j(t)]$$
$$+ b_0(1 - \sum_j \lambda_j(t))$$

a duality relation yielding the output growth frontier:

$$\Delta y_h(t)/y_h(t) = \beta_0^* + \sum_i \beta_i^* (\Delta x_{ih}/x_{ih})$$

where $\beta_i^* = b_i^*/a^*$, $\beta_0^* = b_0^*/a^*$, b_i^* and a^* being nonnegative and b_0^*, β_0^* free in sign. Here b_0^* provides a nonparametric measure of technological progress when it is positive and technological regress, when it is negative. Since the scale S is measured here by $S = \sum_{i=1}^m \beta_i^*$ and the model assumes VRS technology, the measure β_0^* of technological progress is not constrained by the assumption of CRS.

For technology-intensive industries such as computers or microelectronics the input and output growth may be measured, e.g., as a four-year average and then the technological progress (regress) estimated over a 15-year period (1985-2000) on a moving average basis. If a firm has the value $\theta^*(t) = 1.0$ for each of the three subperiod, then its growth efficiency may be said to be *persistent*. Furthermore by considering, e.g., four-year averages one could obtain nonparametric estimates of the long run changes in the technology parameters $\beta_0^*(\tau)$, where τ denotes a four-year sub period, e.g., if $\beta_0^*(1) > \beta_0^*(2) > \beta_0^*(3) > 0$ then the technology is progressing. Likewise the changes in scale $S(\tau) = \sum_{i=1}^{m} \beta_i^*(\tau)$ over sub periods may be estimated by this nonparametric approach.

Two other implications of the growth efficiency model (5) may be briefly noted here. One is the impact of efficiency growth on the market share of efficient firms in the industry. As the industry matures, the growth efficient firms survive and grow, while the inefficient and unprofitable firms leave. Hence the model predicts a positive relation between concentration and efficiency. This hypothesis is closely related to the survivor technique suggested by Stigler (1958) and applied by others, e.g., Rogers (1993). This survivor technique hypothesizes that only the efficient size firms will survive in competition with other plants.

The second implication of model (5) is that it can be transformed to an overall cost efficiency model, when price data are available for the inputs. Let $C_j(t)$ denote total costs for each firm j and let $\tilde{C}_j(t)$ denote its percentage change. Then one could formulate a dynamic nonparametric model as

Min $\phi(t)$

s.t. $\sum_{j=1}^{N} \tilde{C}_j(t)\mu_j(t) \le \phi(t) \tilde{C}_h(t)$ \hfill (8)

$\sum_{j} \tilde{y}_j(t)\mu_j(t) \ge \tilde{y}_j(t)$

$\sum \mu_j(t) = 1, 2, \ldots, N$

This yields the dynamic cost frontier for an efficient firm h when $\phi^*(t) = 1$ and

$$\tilde{C}_h(t) = \gamma_0^* + \gamma_1^* \tilde{y}_h(t) \qquad (9)$$

If $\gamma_0^* < 0$ then there is a downward shift of the cost frontier representing cost efficiency improvement through technological progress. For $\gamma_0^* > 0$ we have technological regress. Note that varying h within the index set $I_N = \{1,2,\ldots,N\}$ the industry can be decomposed into two groups of firms: one comprising the efficient firms with $\phi^*(t) = 1$ for one or more $t = 1,2,...,T$ and the other comprising inefficient firms. If any firm maintains growth efficiency for most of the period T, then its efficiency may be said to be persistent. Once again the survivor technique may be applied here. One useful extension of the linear cost frontier (9) is to adjoin a nonlinear constraint to the LP model (8) as

$$\sum_{j=1}^{N} \hat{y}_j^2(t)\mu_j(t) = \hat{y}_h^2(t) \tag{10}$$

an equality, so that its Lagrange multiplier is unrestricted in sign. The cost efficiency frontier now reduces to

$$\tilde{C}_h^*(t) = \gamma_0^* + \gamma_1^* \tilde{y}_h(t) + \gamma_2^* \tilde{y}_h^2(t)$$

where γ_2^* is unrestricted in sign. Clearly when γ_2^* is negative, then output growth may lead sometimes to a decline in marginal rate of costs, i.e.,

$$\partial \tilde{C}_h^{(t)} / \partial \tilde{y}_h(t) < 0, \text{ if } \tilde{y}_h(t) > \gamma_1^* / |2\lambda_2^*|$$

this may happen due to the so-called "learning curve" effect as the mature firms gain more experience. One may also derive a similar result by using cumulative output $y_j^C(t)$ as another variable affecting costs and therefore prices. Let $c_j(t)$ be average cost per unit of output, $y_j^C(t)$ be the cumulative output. Then one formulates the nonparametric model

Min $\phi(t)$

s.t. $\sum_{j=1}^{N} \tilde{C}_j(t)\mu_j(t) \leq \phi(t)\tilde{C}_h(t)$

$\sum_j y_j(t)\mu_j(t) \geq \tilde{y}_j(t)$

$\sum_j \tilde{y}_j^C(t)\mu_j(t) = \tilde{y}_h^C$

$\sum_j \mu_j(t) = 1; j = 1,2,...,N; t = 1,2,...,T$

The dynamic cost frontier for an efficient firm would then appear as follows:

$$\tilde{c}_h^*(t) = \delta_0^* + \delta_1^* \tilde{y}_h(t) - \delta_2^* \tilde{Y}_h^c(t)$$
$$\delta_0^*, \delta_1^* \geq 0, \delta_2^* \text{ free in sign}$$

Clearly the growth of cumulative output representing cumulative experience as in learning by doing models may generate a reduction in average costs in the long run and hence a reduction in price if the parameter δ_2^* has a positive sign. In the US computer industry the efficient firms have succeeded in reducing average prices by more than 15 percent per year as the empirical study by Jorgenson and Stiroh (2000) shows. Norsworthy and Jang (1992) also found a significant degree of learning curve effects.

5.1 Sales Growth and Decline

Productivity growth and efficiency changes in the US computer industry have been the main focus of research in many recent studies of the high-tech industries like microelectronics, computers, semiconductors and telecommunications. Norsworthy and Jang (1992) are probably the first to provide a detailed empirical study of the US computer industry comprising mainframe, mini and microcomputers (PCs) over three sub periods 1959-67, 1967-75 and 1975-81 and the whole period 1959-81. They estimated a translog total cost function by nonlinear maximum likelihood and measured scale economies and technological progress. In a modified and simplified version (with fixed factor prices) their translog cost function appeared as follows:

$$\ln TC = b_0 + b_1 \ln y(t) + b_2 T \qquad (11)$$

Here T is a time trend variable used as a dummy for the state of technology. Cumulative output or cumulative R&D investment has also been suggested as a proxy for technological change. The inverse of the parameter b_1 can be interpreted as the degree of returns to scale. Hence $1/b_1$ must equal one if there is CRS. The Hicks-neutral technical change is defined by a pure shift of the cost function that leaves the factor shares unchanged. The average annual shift in the cost function is therefore b_2. On differentiating (11) one obtains

$$\Delta TC/TC = b_1(\Delta y/y(t)) + b_2$$

The estimate for b_2 turns out to be (-0.0369) for the whole period 1959-81, whereas $\hat{b}_1 = 0.3477$ and both are significant at 10% level. This suggests that the long run average rate of technical change (or progress) is 3.69% per year in the US computer industry over 23 years 1959-81 and the degree of return to scale (S) is $1/\hat{b}_1 = 2.876$. Both are substantial. The technical change for the three sub periods 1959-67, 1967-75 and 1975-81 were –0.037, -0.051 and –0.041 suggesting no definite trend, although when production workers (b_{2L}) and nonproduction workers (b_{2N}) are used as explanatory variables, the degree of production-worker saving decreases through time from $\hat{b}_{2L} = -0.011$ in 1959-67 to $\hat{b}_{2L} = -0.004$ in 1975-81.

The technological developments in the US computer industry since 1981 have followed two distinct patterns in the new information age. One is the important role of R&D investment in both human capital and shared investment network. The theory predicts that technical uncertainties in R&D investment outcomes can be hedged considerably by pursuing multiple conceptual approaches in parallel. Parallel as opposed to serial exploration of alternative concepts reduces the expected time to successful project completion but raises R&D costs but this can be considerably reduced by sharing and networking. The US computer industry has played a dynamic role in this connection due to the stiff challenges from abroad and rapid growth of international trade. Scherer (1992) has traced this aspect of transmission of R&D competition in the field of international trade. The second important trend in the US computer industry is the pattern of product cycle and its changes over time in recent years. Thore et al. (1996) have argued that in the computer industry the survival of the fittest depends on the need for a company (firm) to bring on line a continuous stream of new products. Each project goes through a typical life cycle of R&D, market introduction, maturation and eventually obsolescence. Two trends are important in this evolution: the market initially expands (this is sometimes called economies of scale in demand, see e.g., Shapiro and Varian (1999)) and competition becomes more intense (this is sometimes called hypercompetition, see e.g., Sengupta (2002)). To supply the expanding market, scale economies and learning curve effects are exploited along with technical progress and this is accompanied by falling prices. Thus many early niche markets in the computer industry such as the markets for laptops or palm PCs have now grown into mass markets. As the manufacturers scramble to shorten the time to market, the R&D and commercialization phase of each cycle becomes shorter. As the products gradually penetrate an ever expanding market, the upswing and maturation phases become longer and longer thus generating accelerated growth.

Costs of manufacturing exhibit significant variations over the product cycle. These costs fall due to learning curve and a significant degree of miniaturization. Thus Touma (1993) estimated annual 5.5% exponential decline of the feature size over the period 1980-91 and a 4% annual exponential decline in the magnetic hard disk head gap spacing.

In the computer industry no company of course stays with a single life cycle due to a rapidly changing technology pattern. The managerial challenge is to bring an optional stream of new 'vintages' of its products and as each company does so, the process of technological evolution continues forward in the industry. Hence the cost and efficiency analysis of firms in this industry have to be analyzed in three phases over the whole period.

Phase 1: rising or maintaining efficiency over time on the average. This may be due to learning by doing, scale economies or changing product-mix, where some component products are still climbing their life cycles.

Phase 2: falling or not maintaining efficiency over time on the average. This may be due to diseconomies of scale, technological regress or product components in their declining life cycles.

Phase 3: time paths exhibiting mixtures of rising and falling or, falling and rising efficiency. This may be due to firms' inability to maintain efficiency up trend due to intense competition and aging product components and/or problems in supply chain management.

Here efficiency is measured in terms of the growth efficiency models formulated in (5) and (6), where $\theta^*(t) = 1.0$ or, $\theta_i^*(t) = 1.0$ for each i would indicate a growth efficient firm in year t. Since our focus is on growth efficiency and not level efficiency, our models and the efficiency calculations based on them are better able to capture the dynamics of the product cycle phases in their rising maturing and declining periods.

The computer industry in US is on the top of the fastest growing sectors in the US economy over the 16-year period 1985-2000. The average sales growth of all the companies in the SIC codes 3570 and 3571 is about 12.8% per year on the average for the period 1985-94, and it is slightly higher (13.1%) for 1995-2000. Some companies like Dell and Silicon Graphics grew much faster over the whole period 1985-2000, e.g., an average of 22.4% per year.

Demand growth involved intense market competition followed by increasing technological diversity with greater utilization of economies of scope and learning by doing. All these resulted in increasing cost efficiency and falling prices.

It is useful to separate the demand growth and rapid technological evolution for analytical purposes. Although demand growth has played a key role in technological evolution, the latter has advanced on its own due to R&D investment in both hardware and software. The dynamic role of R&D investment in the companies on the leading edge of competition had dramatically improved the performance of computers and their diverse range of applications in almost all the manufacturing industries. Technology in new hardware improved due to the development of new software and the latter developed at a rapid rate due to demand from domestic and international users.

Three aspects of the evolution of demand are important in the growth of the computer sector. One is the increase in volume of demand due to globalization of trade. The expansion of international trade in both hardware and software markets has been spearheaded by the rapid advance of software development by the subsidiaries of leading US companies in Asian countries like Taiwan, Korea, Singapore and India. The second aspect of demand growth is due to the significant economies of scale in demand rather than supply. The elasticity of demand with respect to total industrial output has exceeded 2.91 over the whole period 1985-2000, whereas the income elasticity of demand has been about 1.92. Since the value of a network goes up as the square of the number of users, demand growth has generated further investment in expanding the networks through interlocking and other linkages in the network economy. The third aspect of demand growth is due to interlinked demand, i.e., transmission of demand from one arena to other arenas. Thus if total demand $D = D_1 + D_2 + D_3$ is made up of three components: $D_1 = D_1(p,y)$ depending on price and income, $D_2(\tau)$ depending on transmission and D_3 due to exogenous shift of the demand function and the first two components are proportional to overall demand, i.e., $D_1 = \alpha_1 D$ and $D_2 = \alpha_2 D$, then overall demand changes as $D = kD_3$ where $k = (1 - \alpha_1 - \alpha_2)^{-1}$ is the demand multiplier. The higher the proportions α_1 and α_2, the greater is the multiplier, e.g., if $\alpha_1 + \alpha_2 = 0.9$, the shift of one unit of D_3 due to the learning curve effect by users leads to a tenfold increase in demand.

The demand pattern may be modeled as a first order Markov process. Net sales data are used as a proxy for demand. These data are obtained from Standard and Poor's Compustat files for the period 1985-2000. Denoting y_t as net sales in years t the model is of the form

$$y_t = \alpha + \beta\, y_{t-1} + \varepsilon_1$$

Since the β coefficient indicates the growth parameter its estimates for some selected firms are as follows:

Table 1. Estimates of Demand Growth and Efficiency

	$\hat{\beta}$	$t_{\hat{\beta}}$	$\bar{R}^2$	$\bar{\theta}^*$
Dell	1.495	41.181	0.994	1.00
Compaq	1.276	28.728	0.988	1.00
HP	1.116	26.664	0.986	1.00
Sun	1.107	31.810	0.990	0.96
Toshiba	1.043	9.480	0.899	0.98
SGI	0.994	9.470	0.899	0.64
Sequent	0.990	9.407	0.897	0.66
Hitachi	0.718	4.607	0.669	0.64
Apple	0.699	4.427	0.650	0.70
Data General	0.721	10.212	0.681	0.59
Avg (22 firms)	1.102	6.172	0.901	0.89

The last column $\bar{\theta}^*$ denotes the average efficiency based on three typical years 1987, 1991 and 1998, when the efficiency model is used in a level efficiency form with nonradial efficiency measure $\theta_i^*(t)$ with $\bar{\theta}^* = \sum_i \theta_i^* /3$ as follows:

$$\text{Min} \sum_{i=1}^{3} \theta_i(t)$$

$$\text{s.t.} \sum_{j=1}^{32} y_j(t)\lambda_j(t) \geq y_h(t)$$

$$\sum_{j=1}^{2} \lambda_j(t) = 1, \lambda_j(t) \geq 0; j = 1, 2, \ldots, 22$$

The total sample here is 22 companies out of 41, since input output data are not continuously available for all firms. The three units considered here are: x_1 = R&D expenses, x_2 = cost of goods sold including manufacturing and selling expenses and x_3 = expenditure on net plant and equipment. Output (y) is net sales. All these data are in current dollars and they have been considered as financial value data representing heterogeneous physical activities. Clearly the sales growth estimates are highly positively correlated with average efficiency estimated by the LP models.

The above sales growth estimates were checked for any serial correlation by DW statistic. If there is no serial correlation, the statistic will be very close to two. For positive (negative) correlation the statistic will approach 4 (zero). All ten selected companies reported above had DW statistics close to two. Hence the hypothesis of positive or negative serial correlation can be rejected.

5.2 Technical Change and Scale Efficiency

For measuring technical change over time we use the nonparametric LP model (7) based on observed data on growth of inputs and outputs for 22 companies in the Compustat data available from Standard and Poor's Databank. R&D expense, net plant expenditure and cost of goods sold inclusive of marketing and administrative costs along with manufacturing and software development expense are the three inputs as before and net sales growth is used as a proxy for demand growth. Inventory cost and cost of lost sales are ignored here. The estimate of β_0^* from model (7) is obtained in Table 2 where the assumption of CRS (constant returns to scale) is not imposed.

The average annual technical progress for the whole period 1985-2000 is about 12.1% for 22 companies and 10.8% for the 10 companies in Table 2. This is much lower than the estimate of 26% for the period 1959-81 obtained by Norsworthy and Jang (1992). Also it is clear from Table 2 that the ten companies selected here exhibit much higher technical progress in the recent period 1995-2000 compared to the earlier period 1985-89. When the CRS technology is imposed, we use the nonparametric model (2) with the additional condition (3) and the estimate for scale adjusted technical change is much higher, i.e., about 21.1% for the whole period 1985-2000 for all 22 companies. This is only slightly lower than the estimate of Norsworthy and Jang. The scale efficiency measurement exhibited in Table 3 shows an average of 1.403 for the whole period for 10 companies and 1.341 for all 22 companies. These estimates of RTS (returns to scale) are much lower than the estimates of Norsworthy and Jang (1992) for an earlier period 1959-81. If we run an ordinary least squares regression with a correction for the intercept term sometimes called COLS (corrected ordinary least squares) then the estimate of the log linear production function yields a value 1.023 for RTS with a R^2 value of 0.989. Thus the regression estimate of RTS is much lower than the nonparametric estimate.

Finally, we have in Table 4 the estimates of nonradial efficiency measures based on the LP model (6), which allows the overall efficiency measures to be decomposed into three components, e.g., R&D, net plant expenditure and cost of goods sold. The importance of R&D input is clearly revealed. Companies that have experienced substantial growth in sales have also exhibited strong efficiency in the R&D input utilization – e.g., Dell, Sequent, Sun and Data General.

The leaders in phase 1 (rising phase) of the growth frontier may be identified by the number of years the company remained efficient on the average. Based on the estimates of nonradial efficiency Dell, Toshiba, Silicon Graphics, Sun and Data General are leaders (6 out of 9 times it retained growth efficiency) but in terms of R&D efficiency only Sun, Silicon Graphics, Sequent and Data General maintained their leadership (4 out of 9 times). Most of the other companies belonged to phase 3, e.g., Apple did not do well for the period 1985-1994, but in the recent period (1995-2000) it picked up the growth efficiency. Similar is the story of Toshiba. Similar is the experience of Silicon Graphics. For the set of 10 companies analyzed here, none stayed in phase 2 (declining) continuously, although from the overall set of 42 companies many did not survive at all, hence we had to include only 22 companies in our comparison data set.

Thus we may conclude that economic efficiency measurement for firms by the nonparametric approach may be made either in terms of input and output levels (i.e., level efficiency) or their relative growth (i.e., growth efficiency). In an economic environment of rapid technical change and intense market competition, growth efficiency reflects more accurately the efficiency ladder. On the average our empirical results showed that the leading growth efficiency companies enjoyed increased market shares in terms of sales growth. Laggards and growth inefficient firms showed poorest sales growth figures. Also the R&D investment expenditure played a very significant role in explaining the efficiency behavior of leading firms.

The overall COLS regression of the log linear production function showed a highly significant value of 0.162 (significant at 1% level of t) for the coefficient of ln R&D expenditure, whereas net plant and expenditure in logs contributed only 0.009 which is not significant at even 5% level of t statistics. It is remarkable that the leaders in growth efficiency invariably exhibited R&D efficiency to a significant degree.

Since competition in market share and the development of R&D are so crucial in the high-tech industry such as computers, our empirical results point to the need for developing an efficiency-based econometric model of competition between the efficient (leaders) and the inefficient (laggards) firms under conditions of market growth and decline.

Table 2. Annual Average Technical Change Based on Scale Unadjusted LP Model

		Technical progress		average
	1995-89	1990-94	1995-2000	1985-2000
Dell	0.042	0.642	0.320	0.335
Compaq	0.024	0.361	0.164	0.183
HP	0.064	0.050	0.107	0.074
Sun	0.050	0.055	0.049	0.051
Toshiba	0.038	0.024	0.105	0.056
SGI	0.062	0.066	0.057	0.062
Sequent	0.022	0.060	0.036	0.039
Hitachi	0.044	0.024	0.107	0.058
Apple	0.030	0.112	0.315	0.152
Data General	0.049	0.110	0.061	0.073

Note: These estimates assume variable returns to scale.

Table 3. Annual Average Scale Coefficients (S) of the Scale Unadjusted LP Models

	1995-89	1990-94	1995-2000	average 1985-2000
Dell	1.618	1.007	1.065	1.230
Compaq	1.607	1.165	0.963	1.578
HP	1.170	1.269	2.011	1.150
Sun	1.161	1.280	0.956	1.466
Toshiba	1.530	1.066	1.989	1.526
SGI	1.016	1.035	1.749	1.267
Sequent	1.653	1.292	1.451	1.465
Hitachi	1.513	1.020	1.991	1.508
Apple	1.587	1.546	0.469	1.534
Data General	1.260	1.278	1.387	1.308

Note: Scale $S = \beta_1^* + \beta_2^* + \beta_3^*$ is defined in model 7

Table 4. Nonradial Average Efficiency Measures $\theta_i^*(t)$ Based on the Growth Efficiency LP Model (7)

	1985-89			1990-94			1995-2000		
	$\theta_1^*(t)$	$\theta_2^*(t)$	$\theta_3^*(t)$	$\theta_1^*(t)$	$\theta_2^*(t)$	$\theta_3^*(t)$	$\theta_1^*(t)$	$\theta_2^*(t)$	$\theta_3^*(t)$
Dell	0.61	0.44	0.47	1.0	1.0	1.0	1.0	1.0	1.0
Compaq	0.40	0.54	0.50	1.0	1.0	1.0	0.33	0.60	0.75
HP	0.49	1.0	0.47	0.55	0.80	1.0	1.0	1.0	1.0
Sun	1.0	1.0	1.0	1.0	1.0	1.0	0.42	0.24	0.67
Toshiba	0.49	0.62	0.72	1.0	1.0	1.0	1.0	1.0	1.0
SGI	1.0	1.0	1.0	1.0	1.0	1.0	0.25	0.25	0.38
Sequent	1.0	1.0	1.0	1.0	1.0	1.0	0.50	0.54	0.48
Hitachi	0.40	0.68	0.65	1.0	1.0	1.0	0.94	0.84	1.0
Apple	0.52	0.69	0.64	0.51	0.44	0.76	1.0	1.0	1.0
Data General	1.0	1.0	1.0	1.0	1.0	1.0	0.48	0.54	0.77

Note: Three inputs are: x_1 = R&D expenditure, x_2 = net plant and equipment expenditure and x_3 = cost of goods sold. $\theta_i^*(t)$ corresponds to x_i for i=1,2,3

References

- Athanassopoulos, A., Thanassoulis, E. (1995): Separating Market Efficiency from Profitability and its Implications for Planning. Journal of the Operational Research Society 46, 20-34
- Charnes, A., Cooper, W.W., Lewin, A., Seiford, L. (1994): Data Envelopment Analysis: Theory, Methodology and Applications. Kluwer Academic Publishers, Boston
- Dreze, J., Sheshinski E., (1984): On Industry Equilibrium Under Uncertainty. Journal of Economic Theory 33, 88-97
- Farrell, M.J. (1957): The Measurement of Productive Efficiency. Journal of Royal Statistical Society, Series A 120, 253-290
- Gabszewicz, J., Michel, P. (1991): Capacity Adjustments in a Competitive Industry. In Equilibrium Theory and Applications. Cambridge University Press, New York
- Gaskins, D.W. (1971): Dynamic Limit Pricing: Optimal Pricing Under Threat of Entry. Journal of Economic Theory 3, 306-322.
- Johansen, L. (1972): Production Function. North Holland, Amsterdam
- Norman, M., Stoker, B. (1991): Data Envelopment Analysis: The Assessment of Performance. John Wiley, New York
- Novshek, W. (1980): Cournot Equilibrium with Free Entry. Review of Economic Studies 47, 473-486
- Sengupta, J.K. (1990): Transformations in Stochastic DEA Models. Journal of Econometrics 46, 109-123
- Sengupta, J.K. (1999): The Measurement of Dynamic Productive Efficiency. Bulletin of Economic Research 51, 111-124
- Sengupta, J.K. (2000): Dynamic and Stochastic Efficiency Analysis. World Scientific, London
- Sengupta, J.K. (2002): Growth and Efficiency in the Computer Industry. Unpublished paper
- Timmer, C.P. (1971): Using a Probabilistic Frontier Function to Measure Technical Efficiency. Journal of Political Economy 79, 776-794

6
Efficiency Under Uncertainty

Production and cost frontiers of a firm or DMU are directly affected by the uncertainty of market demand and market prices. Randomness in demand may generate unintended shortages or inventories and uncertain prices may induce risk aversion for firms or DMUs, which attempt to choose optimal inputs and outputs. These two types of uncertainty require us to extend the convex hull method of DEA for determining production or cost frontiers.

Another important class of uncertainty is posed by the volatility of the financial markets, where the DMUs are decision makers, who have to make optimal investment allocation decisions. Price fluctuations in capital markets lead to variability of net returns of portfolios or mutual funds, which are mixtures of various individual stocks with varying degrees of volatility. Clearly the convex hull method of DEA model can be applied in this framework and compared with the mean variance theory underlying the capital market model (CAPM). In this chapter we deal with these two types of uncertainty e.g., uncertainty in demand and cost and the uncertainty in investment markets.

6.1   Cost and Demand Uncertainty

Consider first a production model with one output (y), m inputs (x_i) and N firms or DMUs. We compare the relative efficiency of firms in choosing the inputs optimally by minimizing total input costs (TC) with given input prices $w = (w_i)$

$$\text{Min } TC = w'x = \sum_{i=1}^{m} w_i x_i$$

$$\text{s.t.} \quad \sum_{j=1}^{N} x_{ij} \lambda_j \leq x_i; i = 1, 2, \ldots, m \qquad (1)$$

$$\sum_{j=1}^{N} y_j \lambda_j \geq y_h; \Sigma \lambda_j = 1; \lambda_j \geq 0$$

Here the reference firm is indexed by h and its relative efficiency is compared with others in the industry. For more than one output the variable y_j would be an n-element vector. Also, if both inputs (x_i) and output (y) are optimally chosen, then the profit (π) oriented model could be defined as

$$\text{Max } \pi = p'y - w'x$$
$$\text{s.t. } X\lambda \leq x; \ Y\lambda \geq y; \ \lambda'e = 1, \ \lambda > 0 \qquad (2)$$

where e is a column vector with each element being one and prime denotes transpose. For simplicity we consider the one output case. Thus consider the LP model (1) and let x_i^* and λ_j^* be the optimal values, where the reference firm h is on the production frontier

$$y_h = \gamma_0^* + \sum_{i=1}^{m} \gamma_i^* x_{ih}; \gamma_0^* = \beta_0^* / \alpha^*, \gamma_i^* = \beta_i^* / \alpha^*$$

which may be derived from the Lagrangean function:

$$L = -\sum_i w_i x_i + \sum_{i=1}^{m} \beta_i (x_i - \sum_{j=1}^{N} x_{ij} \lambda_j)$$
$$+ \alpha (\Sigma y_j \lambda_j - y_h) + \beta_0 (1 - \Sigma \lambda_j)$$

In case of model (2) with both prices determined by competitive markets one obtains the optimal vectors x* and y*, so that inefficiency exists for a firm j, if $x_{ij} > x_i^*$ or $y_{rj} < y_r^*$.

Next we consider a cost frontier model where all costs are combined as C_j for firm j with components C_{ij} denoting costs of labor, materials and equipment services. This type of model is useful in specifying a cost frontier rather than a production frontier. Two distinct uses of this cost frontier approach may be mentioned here. One is that this frontier may be used to derive an average cost frontier by minimizing which the most efficient scale of output can be determined. Secondly, the role of component costs in the overall efficiency can be more directly evaluated, e.g., costs of R&D expenditure may have learning by doing effects, not shared by other input costs.

By using this cost frontier approach the input oriented DEA model may then be set up as

$$\text{Min } \theta$$
$$\text{s.t. } \sum_{j=1}^{N} C_{ij} \lambda_j \leq \theta C_{ih}; \sum_{j=1}^{N} C_j \lambda_j = C_h \qquad (3)$$

$$\Sigma\lambda_j = 1, \lambda_j \geq 0; j = 1,..., N$$

where DMU_h is tested for efficiency relative to all other DMUs. If the optimal values λ_j^*, θ^* are such that $\theta^* = 1.0$ and all slack variables are zero, then DMU_h is cost efficient in the sense

$$\sum_{j=1}^{N} C_{ij}\lambda_j^* = C_{ih}; i = 1, 2,..., m$$

and $\quad \Sigma C_j \lambda_j^* = C_h$

By duality this implies that if DMU_j is on the cost frontier, it must satisfy the condition

$$C_j = \gamma_0^* + \sum_{i=1}^{m} \gamma_i^* C_{ij}; \gamma_0^* = \beta_0^*/b^*, \gamma_i^* = \beta_i^*/b^* \qquad (4)$$

where b is the Lagrange multiplier associated with the constraint $\sum_j C_j \lambda_j = C_h$. One may also rewrite the model in a form where each DMU is choosing the inputs x_i optimally. Let $c_{ij}x_{ij}$ denote C_{ij}. The model then takes the form

$$\text{Min TC} = \Sigma q_i x_i$$
$$\text{s.t.} \quad \sum_{j=1}^{N} c_{ij}x_{ij}\lambda_j \leq c_i x_i; \sum_j C_j \lambda_j = C_h \qquad (5)$$
$$\Sigma\lambda_j = 1, \lambda_j \geq 0; j = 1, 2,..., N$$

where it is assumed that the input price q_i equals the average input cost $\bar{c}_i$. The cost frontier in this case for DMU_j must satisfy the conditions:

$$\beta_i^* = \bar{c}_i = q_i$$
$$C_j = \gamma_0^* + \sum_{i=1}^{m} \gamma_i^* c_{ij} x_{ij} \qquad (6)$$

Another form of the cost frontier is generated when the cost output relation is considered, e.g.,

$$\text{Min } \theta$$

$$\text{s.t.} \quad \sum_{j=1}^{N} C_j \lambda_j \leq \theta C_h; \sum_j y_j \lambda_j \geq y_h \tag{7}$$

$$\sum_j \lambda_j = 1; \lambda_j \geq 0, j = 1, 2, ..., N$$

If DMU_j is efficient here, then it follows by duality that it is on the cost output frontier defined by

$$C_j^* = (\beta_0^* / \beta^*) + (\alpha^* / \beta^*) y_j \tag{8}$$

where the Lagrangean is

$$L = -\theta + \beta(\theta C_h - \sum_j C_j \lambda_j) + \alpha(\sum_j y_j \lambda_j - y_h) + \beta_0 (\Sigma \beta \lambda_j - 1)$$

If we add a second order output constraint to (7) as

$$\sum_{j=1}^{N} y_j^2 \lambda_j \geq y_h^2 \tag{9}$$

then the cost output frontier becomes quadratic

$$C_j^* = \gamma_0^* + \gamma_1^* y_j + \gamma_2^* y_j^2 \tag{10}$$

where $\gamma_0^* = \beta_0^* / \beta^*, \gamma_1^* = \alpha^* / \beta^*$ and $\gamma_2^* = \alpha^* / \beta^*$, with a* as the nonnegative Lagrange multiplier of the output constraint (9).

The quadratic cost frontier (10) has two advantages over the linear frontier (8). First, it is more flexible since marginal cost varies as output varies. Secondly, one may further minimize the average cost for the efficient DMU_j:

$$AC_j^* = C_j^* / y_j = \frac{\gamma_0^*}{y_j} + \gamma_1^* + \gamma_2^* y_j \tag{11}$$

On minimizing this AC_j one obtains the optimal size of output (y_j^{**}) defining the most efficient scale as:

$$y_j^{**} = \left(\gamma_0^* / \gamma_2^*\right)^{1/2}$$

with

$$c_j^{**} = \min AC_j^* = \gamma_1^* + \left(\gamma_2^* / \gamma_0^*\right)^{1/2} \qquad (12)$$

Clearly the observed average cost (c_j^*) and output (y_j^*) on the frontier would satisfy the inequalities:

$$y_j^{**} > y_j^* \text{ and } c_j^{**} < c_j^* \qquad (13)$$

This implies that demand for firm j must be high enough for producing y_j^{**} to meet demand. Thus with a lower demand the firm would supply y_j^*, but a higher demand would generate a higher supply y_j^{**}.

Now we consider the role of demand uncertainty in the DEA models introduced above. Consider first the cost-minimizing model (1) where demand for output is r and it is random; also the input supply is z_i and it is random. We have to replace the objective function in (7) by the expected total cost, since output demand and input supply contain random fluctuations. Let $f(r)$ and $f(z_i)$ be the probability density functions of demand r and supply z_i with $F(r)$ and $F(z_i)$ denoting their cumulative distributions. Then the DEA model can be transformed as

$$\text{Min ETC} = \sum_i q_i \left[a_i \int_{x_i}^{\infty} x_i f(z_i) dz_i + b_i \int_0^{x_i} z_i f(z_i) dz_i \right]$$

$$+ g \int_0^{y} (y-r) f(r) dr + h \int_y^{\infty} (r-y) f(r) dr \qquad (14)$$

s.t. $\sum_{j=1}^{N} x_{ij} \lambda_j \leq x_i; 1, 2, ..., m$

$$\sum_j y_j \lambda_j \geq y; \Sigma \lambda_j = 1, \lambda_j \geq 0; j = 1, 2, ..., N$$

Here the unit inventory costs are a_i and g and the cost of lost sales and the input shortfall are h and b_i respectively. These parameters are assumed to be known by each firm. The optimal inputs and output are now determined as

$$x_i^* = F^{-1}(\delta_i), \delta_i = 1 - (\beta_i^* / a_i q_i)$$
$$y^* = F^{-1}(\phi), \phi = (g+h)^{-1}(\alpha^* + h) \quad (15)$$
$$\alpha^* y^* = \beta_0^* + \sum_{i=1}^{m} \beta_i^* x_{ij}$$

Clearly higher inventory costs would tend to reduce optimal levels of output and input use. The gaps $|x_{ij} - x_i^*|$ and $|y_j - y^*|$ would indicate inefficiency in input usage and output production respectively.

Two implications of these results are to be noted. First, the presence of expected inventory costs and costs of shortage would affect the DEA efficiency results derived under a deterministic framework. This may explain why some firms may carry large 'organizational slacks' on the average and may then be judged as inefficient in the deterministic DEA approach. Secondly, the form of the distribution of demand for output and supply of inputs would affect the level of expected inventory or shortage carried by firms.

Consider now the transformation of the quadratic cost model specified by (7) and (8) when only demand uncertainty is present:

Max $E(p \min(y,r)) - wC$
s.t. $\sum_j C_j \lambda_j \leq C; \Sigma y_j \lambda_j \geq y, \Sigma y_j^2 \lambda_j \geq y^2; \Sigma \lambda_j = 1, \lambda_j \geq 0$

where $w = 1.0$ and r is random demand with a distribution $F(r)$. The optimal output and the cost frontier can be easily calculated as follows for an efficient DMU_j:

$$C_j = \gamma_0 + \gamma_1 y_j + \gamma_2 y_j^2; \gamma_0 = \beta_0^* / \beta^*, \gamma_1 = \alpha^* / \beta^*, \gamma_2 = a^* / \beta^*$$
$$2a^* y^* + pF(y^*) + \alpha^* - p = 0$$

If the demand r is uniformly distributed with range $0 < r < k$, then the optimal output reduces to

$$y^* = (2a^* + p/k)^{-1} (p - \alpha^*); \quad p > \alpha^* \tag{15}$$

where the Lagrangean is

$$L = E[p \min(y,r)] - C + b(C - \Sigma C_j \lambda_j) + \alpha(\Sigma y_j \lambda_j - y) + \beta_0 (\Sigma \lambda_j - 1)$$

For the linear cost output relation $\gamma_2 = 0$ and we obtain

$$F(y^*) = 1 - \alpha^*/p; \quad y^* = F^{-1}(1 - \alpha^*/p) \tag{16}$$

If for example the demand has an exponential distribution with parameter $\lambda = 1/E(r)$, then (16) reduces to

$$y^* = \ln(p/\alpha^*) \, \bar{r}, \quad \bar{r} = Er$$

Thus the level of optimal output rises as mean demand $\bar{r}$ or price rises and it falls when the implicit cost (α^*) of output inefficiency rises.

Two comments are in order here. First, the risk aversion factor for each firm can be included here by minimizing for example a linear combination of expected total cost and variance of total cost in the DEA formulation (14). However this would impart a higher degree of nonlinearity in the efficiency frontier. Secondly, the firms have no control on the fluctuations of demand and input supply, since we are assuming a competitive market with firms as price takers. In imperfectly competitive markets however price p will vary in relation to demand and thus the price elasticity would affect the optimal levels of output and inputs for instance.

Dynamic Models Under Uncertainty

We consider here two types of dynamic models under uncertainty. One follows a production scheduling model known as the HMMS model due to Holt, Modigliani, Muth and Simon (1960), well known in operations research literature. Here we assume demand uncertainty only and each firm is assumed to maximize an intertemporal net expected return function defined as expected revenue minus expected input and inventory costs over time. The second model assumes that each firm has incomplete knowledge of the inputs and output in the current period t and it has to decide on the levels of optimal inputs and output. Clearly the efficient firm in this framework has two options. One is to forecast the current levels of input and output on the basis of past levels and then use a DEA model to compute an efficiency frontier. The second option is to use last period's inputs and output as observed data and then estimate the optimal production frontier in the current period under demand uncertainty. These two cases would be discussed here.

The first type of dynamic model in a DEA framework has the following intertemporal form:

$$\text{Max } J = \sum_{t=1}^{T} [Ep(t)\{\min(y(t),\tilde{r}(t))\} - EC(I(t),I(t-1)) - \sum_{i=1}^{m} q_i(t)x_i(t)]$$

Subject to the constraint set R defined by

$$I(t) = I(t-1) + y(t) - \bar{r}(t) : I_0 \text{ given}$$

$$\sum_{j=1}^{N} x_{ij}(t)\lambda_j(t) \leq x_i(t), i = 1,...,m$$

$$\sum_{j=1}^{N} y_j(t)\lambda_j(t) \geq y(t) \qquad (17)$$

$$\sum_{j} \lambda_j(t)I_j(t) \leq I(t)$$

$$\sum_{j} \lambda_j(t) = 1; \lambda_j(t) \geq 0; j = 1,2,...,N, t = 1,2,...,T$$

Here $\bar{r}(t)$ is random demand for output with a fixed distribution $F(r)$ with mean $\bar{r}$, E is expectation and the inputs $x_i(t)$, inventory $I(t)$ and output $y(t)$ are optimally chosen for the efficient firm. The prices $p(t)$ and $q_i(t)$ are given. The expected inventory costs are of the HMMS form:

$$EC(I(t),I(t-1)) = 1/2I(t) - \hat{I}(t))^2, \hat{I}(t) = k\bar{r}(t)$$

with $\hat{I}(t) = k\bar{r}(t)$ as the target level of inventory viewed as a proportion of mean demand. On using the Lagrangean function

$$L = J + s(t)\{I(t) - I(t-1) - y(t) + \bar{r}(t)\}$$

$$+ \sum_{i=1}^{m} \beta_i(t)\{x_i(t) - \sum_{j} x_{ij}(t)\lambda_j(t)\}$$

$$+b(t)\{I(t) - \sum_j I_j(t)\lambda_j(t)\} + \alpha(t)\{\sum_j y_j(t)\lambda_j(t) - y(t)\}$$
$$+ \beta_0(t)\{1 - \sum_j \lambda_j(t)\}$$

and applying the Euler-Lagrange conditions it follows that the optimal efficiency frontier for firm j must satisfy for each t=1,2,…,T the following necessary conditions for positive levels of y*(t), $x_i^*(t)$ and I*(t):

$$p(1 - F(y^*)) = s^*(t) + \alpha^*(t); \beta_i^*(t) = q_i(t)$$
$$I^*(t) = k\bar{r}(t) + b^*(t) - s^*(t+1) + s^*(t)$$
$$\alpha^*(t)y_j(t) = \beta_0^*(t) + \sum_{i=1}^m \beta_i^*(t)x_{ij}(t) + b^*(t)I_j^*(t) \qquad (18)$$
$$I^*(t) = I^*(t-1) + y^*(t) - \bar{r}(t)$$

where asterisks indicate optimal values. Several implications follow. First of all, price equals the marginal costs of lost sales, inventories and output in the form of shadow prices. Optimal inventories at time t depend on the target or desired level $\hat{I}(t)$ of inventories, the shadow price of inventories and the change $\Delta s^*(t) = s^*(t+1) - s^*(t)$ in the shadow price of incremental inventories $\Delta I(t) = I(t) - I(t-1)$. This implies that firms with higher desired levels of $\hat{I}_j(t)$ will carry higher optimal inventories and hence have higher inventory costs. Secondly, if these conditions (18) hold for any j over all t, then an optimal recursive decision rule for each of the optimizing variables $z^*(t) = (y^*(t), x_i^*(t), I^*(t))$ can be constructed as a linear function of $z^*(t-1)$ and $\sum_{i=0}^{T-1} u_i \bar{r}_{t+i}$, where u_i is a function of the parameters already computed and $\bar{r}_{t+1}$ is the forecast level of mean demand at time t+i. The advantage of this optimal linear decision rule is that it allows a sequential revision of policies over time as the precision of forecasting of demand improves. Finally, the relative inefficiency of any firm h can be estimated as in the DEA model, i.e., output shortfall below the optimal or excess inputs over the optimal level.

Next we consider the uncertainty associated with incomplete information available to each DMU at time t. Here we assume that each DMU wants to select the optimal inputs $x_i(t)$ and output y(t) at the current time t, given the information at time t-1. The DEA model is of the form

$$\text{Min TC} = \sum_{i=1}^{m} \hat{q}_i(t) x_i(t)$$

s.t.
$$\sum_{j=1}^{N} \hat{x}_{ij}(t) \lambda_j(t) \le x_i(t)$$

$$\sum_{j=1}^{N} \hat{y}_j(t) \lambda_j(t) \ge y(t) \tag{19}$$

$$\Sigma \lambda_j(t) = 1; \lambda_j(t) \ge 0; j = 1, 2, ..., N$$

Here the hat over a variable denotes its forecast from the past levels. Assuming a Markovian framework we assume the forecasts to be generated by an exponentially weighted scheme (EWS) as follows:

$$\hat{z}(t) = \hat{z}(t-1) + v[z(t-1) - \hat{z}(t-1)]; 0 < v < 1 \tag{20}$$

where $z(t)$ may denote any of the variables $q_i(t)$, $x_{ij}(t)$ and $y_j(t)$ above. It is important to note two important features of the EWS of generating forecasts. First, the forecast value $\hat{z}(t)$ may be viewed as the weighted average of past value $z(t-1)$ and its forecast at t-1, i.e., $\hat{z}(t) = vz(t-1) + (1-v)\hat{z}(t-1)$. Secondly, one could rewrite (20) in the form

$$\hat{z}(t) = \sum_{i=1}^{\infty} v(1-v)^{i-1} z(t-i)$$

$$= \sum_{k=1}^{\infty} w_k z(t-k), w_k = v(1-v)^{k-1} \tag{21}$$

where the weights w_k attached to past values decrease exponentially. Note that if v is close to one, the recent observations get more weight so that in the limit v = 1.0 when the past observations have no influence on the forecast values. If v is small, then the past values are important. Clearly the EWS yields smoothed input output data with reduced noise when compared with the observed data containing fluctuations. Hence the DEA model (19) with optimal estimates of $x_i^*(t)$, $y^*(t)$ would yield a more stable production frontier.

The generality of this smoothing approach may be seen by applying this EWS to the cost efficiency model defined by (7) and (9) by replacing C_j, y_j

and λ_j by $\hat{C}_j(t), \hat{y}_j(t)$ and $\lambda_j(t)$ respectively. The smoothed efficiency frontier for DMU$_j$ may then be derived as:

$$\hat{C}_j^*(t) = \tilde{\gamma}_0^* + \tilde{\gamma}_1^* \hat{y}_j(t) + \tilde{\gamma}_2^* y_j^2(t)$$

This frontier may be compared with the frontier (10) derived from observed data. Secondly, the optimal weights v* may be different from the inputs and output and one could select different values of v to simulate the cost efficiency frontier. Thus the sensitivity of the DEA efficiency frontier may be directly evaluated.

Price Uncertainty

Now we consider randomness in prices, which arises in many industries like agriculture. Two types of cases may arise. In one the probability distribution of prices is either known or estimable from past observations. In the second case the probability distribution is either unknown, or inestimable because the sample size is very small.

In the first case we consider an input-oriented DEA model with an expected loss function $EL(q'x)$, where the means $\bar{q}$ and variances v of the vector q are known or estimated.

$$\text{Min } EL(q'x)$$
$$\text{s.t. } \sum_{j=1}^{N} X_j \lambda_j \leq x \quad (22)$$
$$\sum_{j=1}^{N} Y_j \lambda_j \geq Y_k; \Sigma \lambda_j = 1; \lambda_j \geq 0$$

of the loss function is assumed to be quadratic, then expected loss could be written as a quadratic function in the unknown vector x. In the dynamic case the reference unit DMU$_k$ or firm k would minimize the expected present value of a quadratic loss function as follows:

$$\text{Min } E_t [\sum_{t=1}^{\infty} \rho^t \{q'(t)x(t) + (\frac{1}{2})(d'(t)Wd(t)$$
$$+ (\frac{1}{2})(z'(t)Hz(t))\}$$

s.t. $\sum_{j=1}^{N} X_j(t)\lambda_j(t) \le x(t); \sum_{j=1}^{N} Y_j(t)\lambda_j(t) \ge Y_k(t)$ (23)

$\sum_{j=1}^{N} \lambda_j(t) = 1, x(t), \lambda(t) \ge 0$

where ρ is a known discount factor and the vectors $d(t) = x(t) - x(t-1)$ and $z(t) = x(t) - \hat{x}(t)$ are deviations with W and H being diagonal matrices representing the weights. Here $\hat{x}(t)$ may denote the input levels desired by the firm e.g., derived on the basis of knowledge of the past levels of demand as in the HMMS model. The quadratic part of the expected loss function above may be interpreted as expected adjustment costs. On using the Lagrange multiplier $\mu(t) = (\mu_i(t))$ for i=1,2,...,m for the first constraint in (23) and assuming an optimal solution with all slack variables zero, the optimal intertemporal path of m inputs $x_i^*(t)$ may be specified as follows:

$$\alpha_i x_i^*(t) = w_i x_i^*(t-1) + \rho w_i x_i^*(t+1) + h_i \hat{x}_i(t)$$
$$- \bar{q}_i(t) + \mu_i^*(t); i = 1, 2, ..., m$$

where $\bar{q}_i$ is the average input price, $\alpha_i = w_i + \rho w_i + h_i$ and it is assumed that all future expectations are realized, i.e., $E_t(x_i(t+1)) = x_i(t+1)$. This last assumption is also called the rational expectations hypothesis, implying a perfect foresight condition, which is frequently used in modern macrodynamic models in economic theory. If this condition is not fulfilled, then this may lead to errors of forecasting future values.

Consider some important implications of this type of efficiency model. First of all, we have a dynamic source of inefficiency when the observed path $X_k(t)$ of DMU_k does not follow the optimal path $X^*(t) = (x_i^*(t))$. Secondly, the myopic optimal value x* computed from model (22) may be directly compared with the intertemporal optimal path $X^*(t)$. Also, the higher the weights w_i and h_i in the diagonals of matrices W and H respectively, the lower would be the optimal input levels x*(t) over time. Finally, the path of convergence to the steady state equilibrium value $\bar{x}_i^*$ may be calculated as

$$\lim_{t \to \infty} x_i^*(t) = \bar{x}_i^*, i = 1, 2, ..., m$$

provided the characteristic roots are stable.

A second type of dynamic model has been discussed by Sengupta (2000), where capital inputs are distinguished from the current inputs and the input prices are subject to random fluctuations.

Next, we consider the case when the distribution of prices is unknown and only a few observations are available. Let Q be the set of observations available for the input price q and the constraint set in (22) is denoted by R, when $(X, Y) \in R$. Let $q_i^- = \min_{q_i \in Q}$ and $q_i^+ = \max_{q_i \in Q}$ be the minimal and max values in the set Q and $\hat{q}_i = \alpha q_i^- + (1-\alpha) q_i^+, 0 \leq \alpha \leq 1$ be their weighted average. One may then set up a minimax class of DEA models by setting α equal to zero:

$$\min_{X \in R} \sum_{i=1}^{m} q_i^+ x_i$$

Denote the optimal solution of this model by (x_i^+, λ_j^+). Clearly for any positive α less than one, we would have

$$\min_{X \in R} \sum_{i=1}^{m} \hat{q}_i(\alpha) x_i \leq \min_{X \in R} \sum_{i=1}^{m} q_i^+ x$$

where $\hat{q}_i(\alpha)$ is $\hat{q}_i$ for $0 < \alpha < 1$. For $\alpha = 1$, $\hat{q}_i(1) = q_i^-$ and hence one could specify a minimax class of DEA models as follows:

$$\min_{X \in R} \sum_i q_i^- x_i \leq \min_{X \in R} \sum_i \hat{q}_i(\alpha) x_i \leq \min_{X \in R} \sum_i q_i^+ x_i$$

Clearly the minimax model $\min_{X \in R} \sum_i q_i^+ x_i$ specifies 'the best of the worst' case scenario. This provides a more robust efficiency solution than the case $\min_{X \in R} \sum_i \bar{q}_i x_i$, where $\bar{q}_i$ is the average price for input i. One could also interpret this type of model as a Bayesian game, where the DM controls the strategies $X = (x_i)$ and the opponent (Nature) chooses the strategies $q \in Q$.

Note that this class of DEA models can be generalized to include outputs $Y = (y_r)$ as the control variables along with inputs $X = (x_i)$. The objective function then becomes a profit function $\pi = \pi(X, Y) = p'Y - q'X$. The DEA model may then specify the best of the worst policy for specifying efficiency $\underset{X, Y \in R}{\text{Max}} \underset{p, q \in W}{\text{Min}} \pi(X, Y; W)$.

6.2 Efficiency in Capital Markets

Investing in capital markets is always risky due to fluctuations in capital asset prices. How does the investor choose an optimal investment portfolio in such a fluctuating market? The modern theory of finance has developed capital asset pricing models (CAPM) to provide some possible answers to this problem. Our objective in this section is to provide a DEA model framework for evaluating the performance of investment portfolio.

The parametric approach to measuring the performance of investment portfolios has recently come under attack on two fronts. One is due to the deficiencies of the traditional Markowitz mean variance theory and the other to the risk reducing impact of lengthening the investment horizon. Thus a number of empirical studies, e.g., Levy (1998) and March (1999) has found the effects of skewness in return distributions to be important in bullish markets. With regard to investment horizon Tobin (1965) and more recently Malkiel (1996) have shown that investors with horizons exceeding six years can increase their portfolio holdings of equity without concomitant increase in risk measured by the return variance. Furthermore, the risk of holding equity in different mutual fund portfolios has been empirically observed to be decreasing as the portfolio horizon increases beyond six years.

To test these hypotheses in a generalized setting we develop here a nonparametric approach to compare the relative performance of different mutual fund portfolios. This nonparametric approach is based on Farrell's convex hull method of efficiency measurement of different firms, which has been recently generalized to a nonparametric approach now called 'data envelopment analysis' (DEA). Based on the costs (inputs) and return (output) of each mutual fund, this approach constructs a convex hull as the efficiency frontier. Since riskiness measured by return variance can be viewed as costs along with other costs such as loads and other transaction costs, the mean variance efficiency analysis can be easily generalized in this framework so as to include skewness of returns and correlations with the overall market represented by such an index as S&P 500. In order to evaluate the effect of lengthening the portfolio horizon in this nonparametric framework we consider two cases: (a) overlapping horizons and (b) nonoverlapping horizons. In the former case the horizon h is moved forward one period at a time, whereas in the latter case the terminal value of return is computed for a fixed h, e.g., with a portfolio horizon of two years, i.e., h = 2, one calculates the terminal value of returns for 1990, 1992, 1994 and so on for a total period of 1988-98.

Our objective in this section is to evaluate the relative effect of performance of a selected set of sixty mutual fund portfolios over eleven years (1988-98). The annual data set is from Morningstar, which also provides estimates of Jensen's alpha (α), and beta (β) of the capital asset pricing model, the estimates of mean return, its variance and the Sharpe index.

Models of Portfolio Efficiency

The nonparametric portfolio efficiency model compares a specific portfolio or mutual fund k with all other funds by constructing a convex hull based on a linear programming (LP) model as follows:

$$\text{Minimize } \theta$$
$$\text{s.t.} \quad \sum_{j=1}^{N} x_{ij}\lambda_j \leq \theta x_{ik}; i = 1, 2, ..., m$$
$$\sum_{j=1}^{N} y_{rj}\lambda_j \geq y_{rk}; r = 1, 2, ..., s \qquad (24)$$
$$\sum_{j=1}^{N} \lambda_j = 1, \lambda_j \geq 0; j = 1, 2, ..., N$$

Here x_{ij} and y_{rj} are the cost and return components of portfolio or fund j and λ_j denotes the unknown coefficients in the convex combination of N mutual funds. Note that the LP model above is a cost oriented version of an optimizing model. One can also optimize on the output space by rewriting the output constraint as $\sum_j y_{rj}\lambda_j \geq \phi y_{rk}$ and changing the objective function to one of minimizing the term ($\theta-\phi$). Since we have here s=1, i.e., return or yield on each fund, we use the cost or input-oriented LP model (24) as above. Denote the optimal solutions of (24) by asterisks. Then if $\theta^* = 1.0$ and the first two sets of inequalities in (24) hold with equality, then the reference portfolio or fund k is 100 percent efficient. If however θ^* is positive but less than one, then the reference fund k is not 100 percent efficient, since it involves excess costs measured by $(1-\theta^*)$ x_{ik} for at least one component cost i=1,2,...,m. For a detailed discussion of this nonparametric method see, e.g., Sengupta (1995, 2000).

The nonparametric approach above has several flexible features, when it is applied to compare the performance of alternative mutual fund portfolios. First of all, one could determine two subsets of funds, one fully efficient and the other relatively inefficient. Then one could separately measure the risk return trade-off and also the impact of skewness and higher moments by a regression estimate. Secondly, the panel data could be utilized for both overlapping and nonoverlapping portfolio horizons to see if lengthening the horizon has any significant impact on the mean variance frontier. Finally, one could compare these results for the efficient funds with those obtained by stochastic dominance tests, which have been recently applied in finance literature, see, e.g., Levy (1998). These stochastic dominance tests are also nonparametric in the sense that they do not assume any specific form for the return distribution like normal.

The mean variance portfolio theory used in the capital asset pricing model solves the quadratic programming problem:

$$\text{Min } \sigma^2(c) = x'Vx$$
$$\text{s.t.} \quad m'x = c; \; e'x = 1; \; x \geq 0 \tag{25}$$

where x is the vector of allocations, c the lower bound on expected return and (m,V) are the mean and variance-covariance matrix of the vector r of returns. Denote the minimum variance solution by $\sigma^{*2} = x^{*'}Vx^*$, where x^* is the optimal solution of (25). Then one can easily show that the minimum variance is a convex quadratic function of average return c as follows

$$\sigma^{2*} = k_0 - k_1 c + k_2 c^2$$

where

$$k_0 = \alpha/(\alpha\gamma - \beta^2), k_1 = 2\beta/(\alpha\gamma - \beta^2)$$
$$k_2 = \gamma/(\alpha\gamma - \beta^2), \alpha = m'V^{-1}m, \beta = m'V^{-1}e$$
$$\gamma = e'V^{-1}e$$

e being a vector of ones and prime denotes transpose and the variance-covariance matrix V is assumed to be positive definite.

In the dynamic setting with a portfolio horizon T we may consider the representative investor to be minimizing the variance of his final wealth W_T subject to the constraints on wealth at time t and other analogous constraints as follows:

$$\text{Min Var } W_T = E(W_T^2) - (EW_T)^2$$
$$\text{s.t. } E(W_t) = c_t \quad (26)$$
$$W_{t+1} = s_t W_t + r_t' x_t; e' x_t = 1, \text{ all } t$$
$$0 \leq t \leq T-1$$

The minimal variance $\sigma^{2*}(W_T)$ then satisfies the dynamic efficiency frontier:

$$\sigma^{2*}(W_T) = (s_{T-1} W_{T-1})^2 \alpha_{T-1} - 2\lambda_T s_{T-1} W_{T-1} \alpha_{T-1} - 2k_T s_{T-1} W_{T-1} \beta_{T-1}$$
$$+ 2\beta_{T-1} \lambda_T k_T + \alpha_{T-1} \lambda_{T-1}^2 + \gamma_{T-1} k_T^2 \quad (27)$$

where s_t is the rate of return on the riskless asset and other terms are defined as follows:

$$\lambda_T = (g_{T-1} \gamma_{T-1} - \beta_{T-1}) / (\alpha_{T-1} \gamma_{T-1} - \beta_{T-1}^2)$$
$$k_T = (\alpha_{T-1} h_{T-1} - \beta_{T-1} g_{T-1}) / (\alpha_{T-1} \gamma_{T-1} - \beta_{T-1}^2)$$
$$\alpha_T = m_T' R_T^{-1} m_T, R_T = E(r_t r_t')$$
$$\beta_{T-1} = e' R_{T-1}' m_{T-1}, \gamma_{T-1} = e' R_{T-1}' e$$
$$g_{T-1} = c_T - s_{T-1} W_{T-1} (1 - \alpha_{T-1}), h_{T-1} = 1 + s_{T-1} \beta_{T-1}$$

If only risky assets are considered and the steady state frontier is derived, then we obtain $\sigma^{2*}(W) = (\alpha\gamma - \beta^2)^{-1}[\alpha - 2\beta c + c^2]$. This is equivalent to the mean variance frontier (25) derived before, as is to be expected, see, e.g., Sengupta (1989) for a detailed derivation.

The mean variance frontier equations in (25) and (27) can be built into the LP model (24) by redefining returns for different horizons and their associated costs of risk measured by their variances. Denote the terminal return for an h-year portfolio horizon from t-h to t by $r_t(h) = (p_t + g_t + d_t)/p_{t-h}$, where d_t is dividend paid and g_t is the capital gains (losses) distributions. For horizons h = 2,4,5 one could compute the mean returns and the risk costs for various mutual fund portfolios and assess their relative performance. Specifically when we group the funds into separate categories such as growth funds, balanced funds and income funds one could test if lengthening the portfolio horizon has any significant impact on the portfolio efficiency. Note that the h-period return $r_t(h)$ on a portfolio with a horizon of h years implies that the investor selects a portfolio at the beginning of period one and then reinvests the terminal value for h periods. Hence one could construct two types of horizons: overlapping and nonoverlapping. We select the nonoverlapping case, as it tends to reduce the autocorrelation of portfolio returns.

The major motivation for lengthening the investment horizon is the so-called equity premium puzzle in finance literature, which shows that equity investments dominate over the Treasury bill return and this premium increases as the portfolio horizon is lengthened. It is true that many investors will update their aspiration levels after observing the realized portfolio returns; hence a fixed wealth level constraint may be too restrictive. However, many pension funds and institutional investments may still be compatible with this constraint.

We define mutual fund portfolios' weak-form efficiency as the funds ability to fully diversify risk within its respective subset of the overall market. Fully diversifying risk means then that the mutual fund portfolio will have the minimum possible variance for a given level of expected return. This idea can be expressed in another way. By definition, the market portfolio contains every available asset in various proportions. In a multiperiod economy the mean return on the market portfolio is nonstationary, i.e., the market exhibits periodic booms and busts. Hence the proportions of assets in the market portfolio change over time. We say that a mutual fund can diversify its nonsystematic risk if the mutual fund manager selects those stocks, which also happen to greatly influence the market portfolio. This reasoning implies that a mutual fund portfolio may or may not be efficient, since its efficiency depends in part on the level of the market. Furthermore the relative performance of different types of funds may vary in terms of mean variance efficiency. The primary focus of this chapter is to provide a nonparametric framework and an empirical support to justify this characterization of mutual fund efficiency. Clearly the convex hull approach for comparing the relative efficiency of alternative funds provides a more general framework for testing if funds achieve full diversification with respect to the market.

Empirical Test of Efficiency

The major focus in this section is the introduction of a nonparametric technique for measuring the portfolio efficiency of mutual funds and the comparison of that technique with the traditional mean variance analysis and also the stochastic dominance tests which have been recently applied in finance literature. It is well known that an investor can reduce the risk of investment by allocating his wealth to a variety of assets. Hence mutual funds are an attractive form of investment for those individuals who do not possess enough wealth to construct a fully diversified portfolio. We select a set of 60 mutual funds out of a larger set of 125 funds. This selection is made on the basis of two considerations: data availability and relative homogeneity. There are many types of mutual funds. This study focuses on four main groups: (a) growth funds which emphasize capital growth (g_t) in their stock composition, (b) balanced funds which place more weight on risk minimization through diversification, (c) income funds which emphasize more on dividends and hence on cash earnings, and (d) technology funds, which play a major role in NASDAQ composite index.

A set of 60 mutual funds out of a total of 120 is selected in our study over eleven years 1988-98. The selection is based on considerations of homogeneity and continuous data availability from the Morningstar reports, which also provide annual estimates of beta of the CAPM, mean return and its variance.

Four types of empirical tests are applied here to measure the relative efficiency of mutual fund portfolios. The first applies convex hull method in the form of an LP model (24) for one-year horizon (1988 and 1989) with mean returns as output and the load, expense ratio, risk and turnover as input costs. Risk here includes only systematic risk, i.e., for each fund we estimate the security market line and estimate β_j as the ratio of covariance Cov (R_j, R_M) with the market return (R_M) to the variance ($\sigma^2_{R_M}$). Thus the risk of fund k is compared with the linear combination of risks of other funds by means of the constraint

$$\sum_{j=1}^{N} \beta_j \lambda_j \leq \theta \beta_k$$

in the DEA model (24). Note that this provides a more meaningful efficiency comparison than in terms of observed risks σ^2_j, which include both systematic and unsystematic risk. This nonparametric method of measuring portfolio performance is better than the two other alternative measures often used in financial economics, e.g., Jensen's alpha and the Sharpe index defined by the ratio of excess return to its standard deviation. The reasons are several: no need for a benchmark portfolio for comparison, no need to exclude transaction costs and no need to assume the normality of return distribution. Moreover the LP model (24) permits the calculation of an efficiency index for each mutual fund, whereas the Markowitz-Tobin method of estimating a parametric mean variance efficiency frontier provides only statistical averages.

The second type of test applies the same convex hull method of model (24) for three nonoverlapping horizons h = 2,5 and 11. In case of h = 2 the years considered are 1989, 1991, 1993, 1995 and 1997, whereas for h = 5 the years are 1991 and 1995. For h = 11 the whole period 1988-98 is considered.

The third group of tests utilizes the results of the first and second group of tests to regress the optimal measure θ^* in model (24) on the various inputs in order to explain the various sources of efficiency or its lack thereof. Here we use nested regression models with dummy variables in order to test if the fund with 100% efficiency ($\theta^* = 1.0$) differ significantly from those with less than full efficiency ($\theta^* < 1.0$). The final group of tests utilizes the data on returns of only the efficient funds for which $\theta^* = 1.0$ for the whole period 1988-98. We then perform a stochastic dominance (SD) test, which considers the entire distribution of returns rather than only the mean and variance. This SD test performs a linear regression to compare in a pairwise sense any two-fund types or, an efficient mutual fund and the overall market for which S&P 500 is used as a proxy. This type of nonparametric test is based on a diversification theorem due to Hadar and Russell (1971) and applied to those funds only which are found to be fully efficient by the convex hull method in (24) with $\theta^* = 1.0$. Here we write the regression equation as

$$E(y|x) = a + bx \qquad (28)$$

where the two nonnegative random variables (i.e., returns) x and y are assumed to have cumulative distributions F and G respectively. If the estimated regression coefficients satisfy

$$a \geq 0, b \geq 1.0 \qquad (29)$$

then it is easy to show that y has first order stochastic dominance (FSD) over x and hence y will be preferred over x by an investor guided by maximum expected utility. If however we have a more restricted set of values for the regression coefficients such as

$$a \geq 0, \ 0 < b < 1, \ a/(1-b) > E(x) \tag{30}$$

where $E(x)=\bar{x}$ is the mean of x, then y has second order stochastic dominance over x. Note that in our empirical application x and y are any two portfolio returns, which are from the efficient set determined by the convex hull method in (24).

The results of the first test are reported in Tables 1 and 2. Here the five inputs are load, expense ratio, turnover, standard deviation of return and the return covariance with the S&P 500 and the two outputs are mean return and skewness. In an earlier study, Sengupta (1996) found that the skewness of asset return distribution had a significant impact on the mean variance frontier of a mutual fund portfolio. Hence skewness representing the so-called 'good news', 'bad news' effects is considered a potential output in the extended convex hull model (24).

Two motivations may be given for including the skewness of returns in the investor's objective. One is due to the nonnormality of the return distribution, which implies that the upswing and downswing from the mean level may be asymmetrical. Secondly, if u(x) is the utility function of a rational investor, then the first three derivatives satisfy the relation: $u'(x) \geq 0, \ u''(x) \leq 0, u'''(x) \geq 0$. The investor's goal of expected utility maximization yields then a three parameter objective function, i.e., the optimal selection should then maximize both the expected return and the skewness as well as minimize the variance.

It is clear from Table 1 that 70% or more of the funds are nonparametrically efficient, while the growth and technology funds have higher efficiency rates. Since mutual fund portfolios are designed to reduce unsystematic risk through diversification, this result is not unexpected. This provides a nonparametric support to the conclusion reached by Ippolito (1989) in his empirical regression study that in an efficient market mutual funds will have a risk adjusted return sufficient enough to compensate for extra costs in the form of loads and expenses for gathering market information.

The details of average slacks in Table 2 show that there is no significant slack in risk (standard deviation of return) and skewness for the balanced, growth and income funds. Also, lengthening the portfolio horizon (i.e., 1988-98) reduces the risk further. Since turnover is an activity involving higher uncertainty, one would expect that it will be a major source of inefficiency. However, the growth fund managers are turnover efficient on the average, although their expense ratio is lower than that of technology and balanced funds. Both technology and balanced funds have high degrees of inefficiency in terms of turnover costs. Lengthening the portfolio horizon (i.e., taking the whole period 1988-98) reduces risk and skewness effects considerably. Also it is clear from Table 3 that the number of efficient funds tends to increase as the horizon is extended. This is more clearly evidenced in case of growth and balanced funds.

The third group of tests uses a nested regression model with a dummy variable D for each coefficient taking the value 1.0 if the fund is 100% efficient and zero otherwise. The model regresses the optimal efficiency measure θ^* on the inputs such as the expense ratio, turnover costs and market beta as risk and also the outputs such as mean returns and skewness. As expected all of the regression coefficients for the inputs for the inefficient funds are negative, while the return coefficients are positive and statistically significant at 5% level. The skewness coefficient is found to be positive indicating a positive relationship between skewness and efficiency. Since efficient funds are more desirable for the investor than the inefficient funds, positive skewness indicating a high probability of returns exceeding the average would be preferable, whereas negative skewness needs to be compensated by higher mean returns. This inference agrees with a similar conclusion reached by Sengupta and Park (1994) for mutual funds data, where the conventional parametric regression method was employed. An alternative way to present the regression estimates of the nested model is to present the estimates separately for the efficient and the inefficient funds. For the whole period 1998-98 the results are as follows:

Fund	Intercept	Load	Systematic risk	Exp.ratio	Turnover	Return	Skewness	R^2
Inefficient	0.86 (t=36.8)	-0.01 (-2.4)	-0.02 (-4.08)	-0.04 (-2.7)	-0.0 (-3.9)	0.03 (5.6)	-0.04 (4.1)	0.91
Efficient	1.00 (4.99)	-0.0 (-2.15)	-0.0 (3.76)	-0.0 (-2.01)	-0.0 (-3.58)	0.0 (5.3)	0.0 (3.5)	0.89

Clearly the respective coefficients are significantly different in a statistical sense and all coefficients are significant at 5% level. The efficient funds on the average exhibit their frontier properties clearly in terms of the zero regression coefficients, each of which being statistically significant at 5% level.

The mean variance frontier estimates for the coefficient funds reported in Table 6 exhibit two features. One is that the regression coefficient of mean return (c) is always negative though not statistically significant, while the coefficient of c^2 is always positive implying strict convexity. Secondly, the growth funds tend to exhibit a stronger degree of convexity. This implies that the mean variance frontiers for different groups of funds may intersect, thus suggesting that one type of frontier may dominate over the other type in the sense of stochastic dominance. For example the technology and communications fund exhibits lower risk in terms of variance than the S&P 500 at mean return level $c \geq 0.30$. Hence this type of fund has a positive probability of beating even the overall market represented by S&P 500. Likewise the technology fund displays lower risk than the growth and income funds at return levels $c \geq 24$ and $c \geq 18$ respectively. This type of stochastic comparison may be more precisely obtained by the stochastic dominance test discussed before. This is presented in the regression test results in Table 7. Two interesting results follow. Technology funds exhibit SSD over growth funds in all three periods; also balanced funds have SSD over growth and income funds. Since this dominance result does not depend on the assumption of normality in return distributions, it is a more general and important result. Furthermore, by the SSD test neither the growth nor the income fund dominates the market (S&P 500 index), though the technology funds have a positive probability of dominating the market index in the SSD sense. Secondly, the returns data used in Tables 6 and 7 are based on those funds, which are found to be efficient by the convex hull model (24) and hence the SSD test provides a second level discrimination for the investor among the alternative efficient funds. The only limitation is that these estimated return data are based on the domain of the observed sample points and they ignore any degree of skewness preference on the part of the investors. For the case of skewness preference, one has to consider the third order stochastic dominance test and the regression analogue of this kind of test is yet unknown.

Thus we may conclude this section by stating two broad results. First of all, the mean variance efficiency hypothesis holds only partially up to a maximum of 75% among the 60 samples examined here. There are significant variations among the four groups of funds. Secondly, even among the efficient funds the technology and communication fund has second-degree stochastic dominance over the growth fund and furthermore it exhibits a positive probability of beating the market in terms of probability dominance. This result is consistent with an earlier study by Dumas and Sengupta (1991), who found empirical support for the hypothesis that some mutual funds tend to dominate the overall market.

References

- Dumas, E.B., Sengupta, J.K. (1991): Nonparametric Tests of Portfolio Efficiency Under Static and Dynamic Conditions. International Journal of Systems Science 22, 1929-1939.
- Hadar, J., Russell, W.R. (1971): Diversification and Stochastic Dominance. Journal of Economic Theory 3, 288-298.
- Holt, C., Modigliani, F., Muth, J., Simon, H. (1960): Planning Production Inventory and Workforce. Prentice Hall, Englewood Cliffs, NJ
- Ippolito, R.A. (1989): Efficiency with Costly Information: A study of Mutual Fund Performance: 1965-84. Quarterly Journal of Economics 104, 1-23
- Levy, H. (1998): Stochastic Dominance. Kluwer Academic, Boston
- March, J.G. (1999): Learning to Be Risk Averse. In J.G. March (ed.). The Pursuit of Organizational Intelligence. Blackwell Publishers, Oxford
- Malkiel, B.G. (1996): A Random Walk Down Wall Street. W.W. Norton, New York
- Sengupta, J.K. (1989): A Dynamic View of the Portfolio Efficient Frontier. Computers and Mathematics 18, 565-580
- Sengupta, J.K. (1995): Dynamics of Data Envelopment Analysis. Kluwer Academic, Boston
- Sengupta, J.K. (1996): Adjustment Costs in Mean Variance Efficiency Analysis. International Journal of Systems Science 27, 551-559
- Sengupta, J.K. (2000): Stochastic and Dynamic Efficiency Analysis: Economics of Data Envelopment Analysis. World Scientific, London
- Sengupta, J.K. and Park, H.S. (1993): Portfolio Efficiency Tests Based on Stochastic Dominance and Cointegration. International Journal of Systems Science 24, 2135-2158.
- Tobin, J. (1965): The Theory of Portfolio Selection. In F. Hahn and F. Brechling (eds.). Theory of Interest Rates. Macmillan, New York

Table 1. Number of Efficient Funds (with $\theta^* = 1.0$)

Fund type	1988	1998	1988-98
Balanced	10	9	8
Growth	13	14	13
Tech. & Comm.	11	14	13
Income	9	8	8
Total	43	45	42
	(71.7%)	(75.0%)	(70.0%)

Table 2. Average Optimal Slacks in Model (24) in 1988 and 1998
(1998 and 1988-89 values in parentheses)

	Load	Expense Ratio	Turnover	Cov. With market	Mean	Skewness
Balanced	0.0	0.25	36.7	3.4	0.0	0.0
	(0.0)	(0.29)	(35.2)	(3.12)	(0.0)	(0.0)
	(0.0)	(0.14)	(30.1)	(2.89)	(0.0)	(0.0)
Growth	1.54	0.24	0.0	13.01	0.40	0.0
	(1.57)	(0.21)	(0.0)	(12.90)	(0.38)	(0.0)
	(1.25)	(0.28)	(0.0)	(10.00)	(0.20)	(0.0)
Tech. & Comm.	0.25	0.41	47.1	8.02	0.52	0.67
	(0.31)	(0.39)	(44.3)	(7.78)	(0.45)	(0.69)
	(0.41)	(0.29)	(40.2)	(6.89)	(0.0)	(0.0)
Income	0.31	0.16	19.24	9.65	0.08	0.07
	(0.39)	(0.14)	(19.01)	(9.54)	(0.06)	(0.10)
						(0.0)

Table 3. Number of Efficient Funds for Different Horizons (h)

	h=2					h=5		h=11
	1989	1991	1993	1995	1997	1992	1997	1998
Balanced	9	10	11	12	13	9	11	12
Growth	12	13	14	14	14	15	15	13
Tech. & Comm.	10	11	12	11	10	12	13	12
Income	8	9	7	8	9	9	9	8

Table 4. Average Optimal Slacks in (a) Mean, (b) Standard Deviation, (c) Load, (d) Turnover for Selected Periods

		1998-92	1993-98	1988-98
Balanced	(a)	0.0	0.0	0.0
	(b)	0.04	0.05	0.0
	(c)	0.0	0.0	0.0
	(d)	38.6	29.2	27.2
Growth	(a)	0.42	0.61	0.51
	(b)	0.0	0.0	0.0
	(c)	1.51	1.72	1.61
	(d)	0.0	0.0	0.0
Tech. & Comm.	(a)	0.51	0.72	0.61
	(b)	0.84	0.98	0.92
	(c)	0.26	0.35	0.31
	(d)	47.6	48.2	34.4
Income	(a)	0.04	0.01	0.0
	(b)	0.0	0.0	0.0
	(c)	0.31	0.52	0.41
	(d)	19.4	21.1	15.9

Table 5. Regression of Efficiency Measure θ^* on the Various Inputs for Selected Years

$\theta^* = a_1 + a_2 D + a_3 \beta + a_4 \beta D + a_5 ER + a_6 ER\ D + a_7 T + a_8 TD + a_9 \mu + a_{10} \mu D + a_{11} SK + a_{12} \sigma^2 SK\ D.$ (D=1 for efficient funds and zero otherwise)

	1988-92	1993-97	1988-98
a_1	0.896	0.901	0.895
	(t=31.2)	(t=25.2)	(t=37.2)
a_2	0.094	.099	0.105
	(32.9)	(36.4)	(37.4)
a_3	-0.089	-0.092	-0.083
	(-4.5)	(-4.1)	(-3.9)
a_4	0.089	0.092	0.083
	(4.2)	(4.0)	(3.3)
a_5	-0.064	-0.061	-0.053
	(-4.4)	(-4.0)	(-4.1)
a_6	0.064	0.061	0.053
	(4.9)	(4.8)	(3.2)
a_7	-0.006	-0.002	-0.001
	(-2.9)	(-2.5)	(-2.3)
a_8	0.0006	0.002	0.001
	(2.8)	(2.8)	(2.03)
a_9	0.014	0.017	0.012
	(6.5)	(6.1)	(5.8)
a_{10}	-0.014	-0.017	-0.012
	(5.9)	(-5.4)	(-5.1)
a_{11}	0.0008	0.0007	0.005
	(4.9)	(4.8)	(4.5)
a_{12}	-0.008	-0.007	-0.005
	(3.8)	(3.5)	(3.2)
R^2	0.898	0.911	0.893
DW	2.064	2.812	2.057

Note: β = market beta, ER = expense ratio, T = turnover, μ = mean return, SK = skewness of returns

Table 6. Regression Estimates of the Quadratic Mean Variance Frontier
$$\sigma^{*2} = k_0 - k_1 c + k_2 c^2$$

	1988-92				1993-97			
	k_0	k_1	k_2	R^2	k_0	k_1	k_2	R^2
Balanced	321.4	23.4	0.60	0.37	341.2	22.9	0.61	0.41
	(t=1.21)	(0.91)	(0.61)		(t=2.4)	(1.12)	(0.72)	
Growth	601.4	22.1	0.64	0.29	685.2	24.2	0.68	0.33
	(t=0.71)	(0.41)	(0.41)		(t=1.20)	(0.51)	(0.90)	
Income	434.1	31.2	0.89	0.29				
	(t=1.21)	(0.61)	(0.67					
Tech. &	702.1	25.4	0.49	0.28	741.2	26.4	0.51	0.34
Comm.	(0.95)	(0.41)	(0.81)		(1.24)	(1.02)	(1.04)	
S&P 500	323.1	5.41	0.28	0.31	361.2	6.92	0.38	0.38
(observed)	(4.81)	(2.41)	(3.41)		(5.10)	(2.29)	(4.12	

	1998-99			
	k_0	k_1	k_2	R^2
Balanced	338.1	22.1	0.58	0.32
	(t=1.08)	(0.47)	(0.44)	
Growth	634.8	20.2	0.60	0.25
	(0.68)	(0.38)	(0.34)	
Income	492.3	94.3	5.04	0.27
	(1.05	(0.75)	(0.62)	
Tech. &	724.0	18.89	0.27	0.21
Comm.	(0.74)	(0.34)	(0.41)	
S&P 500	344.4	6.87	0.33	0.31
(observed)	(5.08)	(2.24)	(3.51)	

Note: t-values in parentheses

Table 7. Regression Tests for SSD for Selected Periods

Period	Dependent Variable	Intercept	Slope	R^2	DW	Remarks
1988-92 G	B	0.269**	0.734**G	0.91	1.79	B SSD G
	B	0.281**	0.751**I	0.83	1.78	B SSD I
	G	0.159	0.860**I	0.69	1.72	G SSD I
	T	1.275**	0.079G	0.72	1.81	T SSD G
1993-97 G	B	0.279*	0.947**G	0.74	2.61	B SSD G
	B	0.291**	0.790I	0.81	2.64	B SSD I
	T	1.164**	0.061*G	0.49	2.34	T SSD G
1998-98 G	B	0.261	0.956**G	0.73	2.63	B SSD G
	B	0.740	0.503T	0.06	1.48	B SSD T
	T	1.154**	0.055*G	0.01	0.81	T SSD G
	I	2.288	0.055B	0.001	0.82	I SSD B

Note: B = balanced fund, G = growth, T = tech. & comm.. fund, I = income fund. One and two asterisks denote significant t-values at 5 and 1% respectively.

7
Input Sharing and Efficiency

In recent times competition has been most intense in the modern technology-intensive industries and R&D investment in knowledge capital has played a pivotal role. Increasingly this type of investment has been subject to inter-firm cost sharing. By pooling R&D resources the firms can exploit economies of scale due to higher scale and then share the productivity gains. Network investment is another area. As Lu (2001) has recently discussed that for many small and medium-size companies the network sharing of resources with similar needs has become critical to business success. Sharing R&D in the Internet economy has also become very common. Sharing communications through satellite systems by different carriers has also been a common phenomenon in the communications industry. In modern growth theory in macroeconomics Lucas (1993) and others have emphasized the scale economies at the industry level e.g., R&D investment and how it spreads through transmission of new knowledge across firms, which then enjoy productivity gains as external economies.

This type of sharing phenomena may sometimes lead to coalition or mergers involving inter-firm cooperation at a horizontal level comprising firms of the same stage of production. Alternatively it may lead to collusive behavior among firms involving cooperation in resource pooling, production or pricing. In the DEA framework we consider these two types of sharing involving interdependence among firms.

In the first case we deal with the production efficiency problem, when it is assumed that firms can form coalitions of different sizes. This immediately leads to a game-theoretic concept of efficiency. The second case considers cost sharing of fixed-capital investment in the common network only. Such a strategy reduces each member firm's variable cost of production, because the cost of the pooled investment in the network is subject to subadditivity.

7.1 Efficiency in the Core

Consider for simplicity one output (y_j) and m inputs (x_{ij}) for each firm j (j=1,2,...,n) and the reference firm k is tested for relative efficiency in terms of the following LP model

$$\min_{\beta} c_k = \sum_{i=1}^{m} \beta_i x_{ik}$$

s.t. $\sum_{i=1}^{m} \beta_i x_{ij} \geq y_j; j = 1, 2, ..., n$ (1)

$\beta_i \geq 0$

If the optimal weights β_i^* are such that $\sum_i \beta_i^* x_{ik} = y_k$ and all other slack variables are zero, then firm k is relatively efficient by the convex hull method. If however $\Sigma \beta_i^* x_{ik} > y_k$, then it is relatively inefficient, since the optimal output y_k^* defined by $\sum_i \beta_i^* x_{ik}$ exceeds the observed output y_k. The above model can easily be generalized to multiple outputs by rewriting the constraints as

$$\sum_{i=1}^{m} \beta_i x_{ij} \geq \sum_{r=1}^{s} \alpha_r y_{rj}; j = 1, 2, ..., n$$

$$\sum_{r=1}^{s} \alpha_r y_{rk} = 1; (\alpha_r, \beta_i) \geq 0$$

Now consider the DEA model (1) as a production game, where the n firms are viewed as n players. They can form coalitions of different sizes. Let the grand coalition of all n players be denoted by a set $N = \{1,2,...,n\}$ and any proper subset of N is denoted by S. Consider the dual of the LP model (1) as follows:

$$\max z = \sum_{j \in S} y_j \lambda_j$$

s.t. $\sum_{j \in S} x_{ij} \lambda_j \leq \hat{x}_i, i = 1, 2, ..., m$ (2)

$\lambda_j \geq 0, j \in S$

We may form the characteristic function v(S) for any coalition S as

$$v(S) = \max \sum_{j \in S} y_j \lambda_j$$

$$\text{s.t.} \quad \sum_{j \in S} x_{ij}\lambda_j \leq \hat{x}_i(S), i = 1, 2, \ldots, m \tag{3}$$

$$\lambda_j \geq 0, j \in S$$

where $\hat{x}_i(S)$ is a particular allocation of input i from the total amount $\sum_{j \in S} x_{ij}$ the coalition has. The total amount may be viewed as the pooled resource available to the group, which decides to allocate it optimally among its members. Let S_r (r = 1,2,...,N) denote the coalition of size r. Thus for r = 1 we have individual efficiency, where there is absence of any collusion, whereas for r = N we have only one firm, a cartel or monopoly.

In terms of the cost oriented LP model (1) we could specify a similar model for a fixed size coalition S_r (1 < r < n):

$$\text{Min } c_k = \hat{x}_k(S_r)'\beta, \hat{x}_k(S_r) = \hat{x}_{ik}(S_r)$$

$$\text{s.t.} \quad \sum_{i=1}^{m} \beta_i x_{ij} \geq y_j, j \in S_r \tag{4}$$

$$\beta_i \geq 0$$

Several incentives exist in many networking situations when, e.g. the n competing firms bid for higher input allocations. One incentive is that by joining a coalition S_r a firm can reduce its costs more than by not joining. A second reason is that some inputs like R&D investment may have significant economies of scale, which may lower the variable costs further. In this case however we may have to introduce a nonlinear cost function. For example the cost c_k in the LP model may be viewed as $c_k = \hat{x}_k(S_r)'\beta(S_r)$, where β_i tends to fall as the total pooled resource $x_i = \sum_{j \in S_r} x_{ij}$ increases. This framework may also be viewed as a firm vs. industry model. Each firm has to be efficient with a given industry price of output. But the industry decides on the optimal number of firms by minimizing the total cost of producing the aggregate output given by the total market demand. This means that some firms may be squeezed out, since other more efficient firms may exist. Finally, the input allocation game defined by the output-oriented model (4) may be used to characterize a nonempty core as defined in game theory.

We consider now the allocation game defined in (4) for a coalition S. One could then specify three types of coalitions as follows:

(a) One player coalitions: $S = S_1$

Here the n players do not cooperate and the minimax equilibrium concept can be employed as a possible solution. Thus, player k assumes all other players playing against his interest and choosing their strategies to maximize his cost c_k defined in (4). Let $\beta(N-1)$ denote the (n-1)-tuple vector with elements $\{\beta(1),\beta(2)\ldots,\beta(k-1),\beta(k+1),\ldots,\beta(n-1)\}$ and B_{N-1} be the feasible set of solutions specifying the admissible strategies. Then $\beta^*(k)$ is a minimax strategy for player k, if and only if for all $\beta(k) \in B_K$ we have

$$\underset{\beta(N-1)}{\text{Min}} c_k(\beta^{**}(k),\beta(N-1)) \leq \underset{\beta(N-1)}{\text{Min}} c_k(\beta(k),\beta(N-1))$$

where $\beta^{**}(k) = \max c_k = \max \hat{x}'(S)\beta$, $\beta(N-1) \in B_{N-1}$ and it is assumed that the cost function c_k in (4) is finite for all the cases considered. This type of solution specifies first the worst-case scenario for player k i.e., the maximal costs due to other players' strategies. Then it chooses the best of the worst. It is clear that if pure strategy saddle point exists for every two-player zero-sum game with cost $c_k(\beta(k),\beta(N-1))$ then the minimax strategy must exist for player k.

(b) n-player coalitions. Here each of n players may agree to cooperate and thereby achieve a lower cost, than he would if all players played their minimax strategies. Here the concept of Pareto optimality is most useful. We define a feasible vector β^* to be Pareto optimal, if and only if for every feasible vector β we have,

$$c_k(\beta) \geq c_k(\beta^*), \text{ for all } k \in \{1,2,\ldots,n\}$$

and for at least one k, $c_k(\beta) > c_k(\beta^*)$.

(c) n-player coalitions (S_r; $1 < r < 1$). Here we have a coalition of r members. Let $\beta(R)$ denote their strategies belonging to a feasible set B_R. The strategies of other players are denoted by $\beta(N-R)$ belonging to a feasible set B_{N-R}. Then the vector $\beta^*(R) = \{\beta^*(1),\beta^*(2),\ldots,\beta^*(r)\}$ is Pareto optimal up to coalition of size r, if and only if we have

$$\Delta c_k = \underset{\beta(N-R)}{\text{Max}} c_k(\beta(R),\beta(N-R)) - \underset{\beta(N-R)}{\text{Max}} c_k(\beta^*(R),\beta(N-R)) \geq 0$$

$$\text{for all } k \in \{1,2,...,r\} \tag{5}$$

and for at least for one k, $\Delta c_k > 0$. Now let P be the set of all possible coalitions S, where S may have different sizes from 1,2,..., up to n. Let $\bar{\beta}^*$ be optimal for each such coalition in P i.e., condition (5) holds for every $S \in P$ (i.e. collective optimality), then the vector $\{c_1(\bar{\beta}^*), c_2(\bar{\beta}^*),...,c_r(\bar{\beta}^*)\}$ belongs to the core.

If the optimality of the Pareto-solution $\bar{\beta}^*$ is unaffected by a certain type of enlargement of the data matrix, then it may be said to be robust for this type of data enlargement. For example, consider three firms with each producing one unit of a single output with the following two inputs (x_1, x_2):

	1	2	3
x_1	2	3	4
x_2	2	2	1

Clearly the second firm is not Pareto efficient, since it is dominated by the first firm requiring less input x_1. Now consider data enlargement in the form of the second column replaced by $(3+\varepsilon, 2+\varepsilon)'$ where ε is a nonnegative random variable. Clearly the optimality of the Pareto solution $\bar{\beta}^*$ would be unaffected.

Some implications of the core concept may now be briefly outlined. First of all, consider two coalitions S and N-S, where N is the grand coalition. The values of the two coalitions are v(S) and v(N-S) as defined before. If the coalition S knows that the value of the grand coalition is v(N), then there may be a positive surplus defined by $[v(N) - v(S) - v(N-S)]$. Following Johansen (1982) one may utilize here the notion of the degree of aggressiveness of coalition S as the share θ_S, which the coalition will aspire to get out of this surplus. Thus the claim of coalition S will be

$$R(S) = v(S) + \theta_S [v(N) - v(S) - v(N-S)] \tag{6}$$

If θ_S is zero for all coalitions, then we have the ordinary core but with $\theta_S = 1$ for all coalitions S we have the maximally aggressive core. For $0 < \theta_S < 1$ we have the intermediate degree of aggressiveness in the core.

Secondly, let Q be any of the three coalitions S, N and N-S and consider the DEA model (3) with S replaced by Q. We can then compute the value of R(S) in (6) above for various values of θ_S that specify different rules of sharing the surplus.

Finally, we may view the DEA model with two stages. In the first stage the subset $n_1 < n$ of firms are determined which are all technically efficient. In the second stage we consider an allocation game among the n_1 firms, where some may be small in terms of output, while others may be big. The industry may select among these n_1 firms by minimizing total costs $C = \sum_{j=1}^{n_1} C_j(y_j)$ subject to the condition that total supply (Σy_j) equals total demand D. Here $C_j(y_j)$ is the cost function of firm j e.g., it may be quadratic and derived from a DEA type of model, as we have discussed before. In this case the efficient allocation of output among the active firms (i.e., those with positive output) makes them all have the same marginal cost i.e., $p = MC_j = \partial C_j / \partial y_j$ with j denoting active firms. Under monopoly or collusion a conscious mechanism secures efficiency because the cartel or the monopolist actively seeks a maximum net return p. An optimal results then there choice of output and an optimal number of active firms, giving the least total cost for the total industry output that maximizes net return. Therefore maximum net revenue and maximum efficiency are consistent under cartel or collusion.

Under competition no inactive firm can obtain a larger net return than the least profitable of the active firms, i.e., those with lowest average costs. This implies a selection of active firms such that price equals minimum average cost. It follows that there is maximum efficiency under competition.

7.2 Shared Investment and Group Efficiency

Consider now a Cournot type market model, where each firm j (j=1,2,...,n) maximizes profit π_j

$$\pi_j = py_j - C(y_j; k_j) \tag{7}$$

where market-clearing price $p = a - b \sum_{j=1}^{n} y_j$ is assumed to be given and $C(y_j;k_j)$ is the long run cost function with k_j as the capacity measured in terms of output. In the short run k_j is constant and assuming linearity the cost function may be written as $C_j = \gamma_{0j} + \gamma_{1j} y_j$ for all $y_j \leq k_j$. This cost function may be derived as a cost frontier for firm j from the cost-oriented DEA model

$$\text{Min } \theta$$
$$\text{s.t. } \Sigma C_j \lambda_j \leq \theta C_h; \Sigma y_j \lambda_j \geq y_h \qquad (8)$$
$$\Sigma \lambda_j = 1, \lambda_j \geq 0; j = 1, 2, ..., n$$

In the long run the capacity output variable k_j also varies at a cost $F(k_j)$ thus affecting the short run cost frontier also. We consider two different ways of introducing the capacity variable k_j. One is to assume that the marginal cost $\gamma_{1j} = \gamma_{1j}(k_j)$ depends on the level of k_j. In many high-tech industries like microelectronics and computers the marginal cost γ_{1j} declines as capacity is increased. Thus the production capacity expansion gives rise not only to economies of scale but also to lower variable cost. This is specified by the functions $\gamma_{1j}(k_j) = v_j/k_j$ and $F(k_j) = g_j \ln k_j$ with $g_j > 0$. The long run profits may then be written as

$$\pi_j^L = (a - b \sum_{j=1}^{n} y_j) y_j - \gamma_{0j} - y_j(v_j/k_k) - g_j \ln k_j$$

whereas the short run profit π_j^S is given by

$$\pi_j^S = (a - b \sum_{j=1}^{n} y_j) y_j - \gamma_{0j} - \gamma_{1j} y_j$$

The short run optimal output is given by

$$y_j^* = (1/2b)(a - \gamma_{1j} - b \sum_{j=1}^{n-1} y_j) \qquad (12)$$

The long run optimal capacity output can be easily obtained by maximizing π_j^L above i.e., by equating to zero the expression

$$d\pi_j^L / dk_j = -y_j(\partial \gamma_{1j}/\partial k_j) - \partial F(k_j)/\partial k_j$$

i.e.,

$$k_j^* = (g_j/v_j)y_j^*$$

Now consider the situation when the n firms agree to pool their fixed capital investments in a common network $K = \Sigma k_j$, where the new fixed cost function is $F(K)$ and each firm's share is $\theta_j F(K)$ where $\Sigma q_j = 1$ and $\theta_j \geq 0$. The joint cost $F(K)$ is assumed to have the feature of subadditivity and economies of scale in the sense

$$\sum_{j=1}^{n} F(k_j) \geq F(\sum_{j=1}^{n} k_j) \tag{13}$$

This assumption is appropriate for many high-tech industries today e.g., by pooling their R&D expenses each firm can save individual costs due to externalities and scale economies. Lu (2001) has discussed in some detail about the implications of pooling resources by high-tech firms. If $\theta_j = 1/n$ then we have equal sharing and the long run profit function then becomes

$$\pi_j^{LR} = \pi_j^L - \frac{1}{n}(g_j \ln K)$$

Its maximization yields the optimal capacity as

$$k_j^{**} = (n^2 v_j/g_j)y_j^*$$

If however the firms do not pool their fixed investment, then we get

$$k_j^* = (v_j/g_j)y_j^*$$

Clearly for $n > 1$, we obtain $k_j^{**} > k_j^*$, where y_j^* is given by (12). Since the marginal cost of capacity investment is decreasing, we have this result that the pooling of resources and sharing the total cost equally would increase the optimal capacity output. Lu (2001) has considered cases other than $\theta_j = 1/n$ and has shown that a pooled model with proportional shares is more efficient in the hence of higher capacity output than a model with equal shares, when economies of scale are moderate at the equilibrium capacity size of an equal-share model.

Next we consider a second way of introducing the capacity output variable and the effect of pooling the capacity investment. We consider an extended DEA model

Min θ

s.t. $\sum_{j=1}^{n} C_j \lambda_j \leq \theta C_h ; \sum_j y_j \lambda_j \geq y_h ;$

$\sum y_j^2 \lambda_j \geq y_h^2 ; \Sigma k_j \lambda_j \geq k_h ; \sum_j k_j^2 \lambda_j \geq k_h^2$

$\Sigma \lambda_j = 1, \lambda_j \geq 0; j = 1, 2, ..., n$

If a firm j is efficient in terms of the DEA model, then its cost frontier can be written as

$$C_j = \gamma_{0j} + \gamma_{1j} y_j + \lambda_2 y_j^2 + b_{1j} k_k + b_{2j} k_j^2 \tag{14}$$

The average cost of capacity output is then

$$AC_j = C_j / k_j = \frac{\gamma_{0j}}{k_j} + b_{1j} + b_{2j} k_j$$

On minimizing this average cost we obtain the optimal capacity output ($\bar{k}_j$) as

$$\bar{k}_j = [\gamma_{0j} / b_{2j}]^{1/2} \tag{15}$$

Now consider the case when each k_j is replaced by $\hat{k}_j = \theta_j \Sigma k_j$ which equals $\Sigma k_j / n$ for equal shares. In this case the optimal capacity output ($\tilde{k}_j$) becomes

$$\tilde{k}_j = [\tilde{\gamma}_{0j} / \tilde{b}_{2j}]^{1/2}$$

So long as $\tilde{b}_{2j} < b_{2j}$ or, $\tilde{\gamma}_{0j} > \gamma_{0j}$ or both, we have the case $\tilde{k}_j > \bar{k}_j$, i.e., optimal capacity output is higher in case of pooling of investments in a common network.

The DEA model for reducing capacity costs may also be presented in an allocative efficiency framework as follows:

$$\text{Min TC} = q'x + C(R)$$

$$\text{s.t.} \quad \sum_{j=1}^{n} x_{ij}\lambda_j \leq x_i; \quad \sum_{j=1}^{n} R_j \lambda_j \leq R \qquad (16)$$

$$\sum_{j=1}^{n} y_j \lambda_j \geq y_h; \Sigma \lambda_j = 1; \lambda_j \geq 0$$

Here $x = (x_i)$ is vector of m inputs with unit costs $q = (q_i)$, R_j is the research input for firm j, y_j is output and $C(R)$ is the cost of research. The optimal values of x and R are to be determined. If the research cost function is linear i.e., $C(R) = wR$, then (16) defines an LP model for evaluating the relative efficiency of firm h. If this firm is efficient then we must have $x_{ih} = x_i^*$ and $R_h = R^*$. But if the research inputs lower the unit costs of production, then the objective function of (16) may be revised as

$$\text{Min TC} = \sum_{i=1}^{m} (q_i - f_i)x_i + wR$$

Where f_i is the marginal reduction of unit production costs q_i. Since f_i depends on R, it is clear that increasing R would imply higher f_i and hence lower net production cost $\hat{q}_i = q_i - f_i(R)$. In the general case the research cost function $C(R)$ is nonlinear and pooling of research inputs by firms help them reduce total costs due to external economies of scale. Let $\hat{R}_j = \theta_j \sum_{i=1}^{n} R_i$, where θ_j is the share of firm j in the total pool of research inputs $R_T = \Sigma R_j$. Then the general form of the allocative efficiency model may be written as

$$\text{Min TC} = \sum_{i=1}^{m} (q_i - f_i(R_T))x_i + C(R)$$

$$\text{s.t.} \quad \sum_{j=1}^{n} X_j \lambda_j \leq x; \quad \sum_{j=1}^{n} \hat{R}_j \lambda_j \leq R \qquad (17)$$

$$\sum_{j=1}^{n} y_j \lambda_j \geq y_h; \sum_{j} \lambda_j = 1; \lambda_j \geq 0$$

Here the research cost function C(R) has the feature of subadditivity and economies of scale. If market prices are available, then the objective function would be modified as Max profits = py(R) - TC and y_h in the constraint replaced by the unknown output level y. The y(R) specifies the dependence of output on research input R. It is clear that this nonlinear program is linear in the vector $\theta = (\theta_j)$ of shares and the constraint set is compact. Hence an optimal vector θ^* exists, which implies that firms which are more cost efficient are given higher allocations of total research fund R_T. As in the allocation game considered before we obtain the optimal allocation rules for group efficiency.

Sharing Knowledge Capital

In modern high-tech industries like computers and telecommunications R&D investment for improving technology has played an active role. This type of investment has significant economies of scale both internal and external. Internally it means that a firm's average cost declines as the size of this investment increases. By pooling such investment the industry can lower its average cost of production. External economies refer to the fact that the expansion of total industry output lowers the total cost curve of each firm or most of the firms in the industry.

In the modern high-tech industries of today the expansion of total industry output may be caused by the rapid growth in global demand due to demand side economies of scale. For example the customers of Microsoft value its operating system because they are widely used in the industry. Unlike the supply side economies of scale, the demand side economies of scale do not dissipate or get exhausted when the market gets larger and larger. In dynamic competition this demand side economies of scale may generate substantial shift of the demand curve upwards. Three aspects of this demand expansion have been increasingly important in recent years. One is the emergence of globalization of trade and the transactions in the Internet economy through e-commerce, e-trade. Adam Smith who emphasized the point that the economies of division of labor is limited by the size of the market strongly favored the role of competitive international trade and its expansion as the prime mover of industrial growth. The second is the growth of total knowledge capital in the industry, which increases the efficiency of labor and other inputs of each firm. Knowledge capital is like innovations of the Schumpeterian world, which are complementary and not rivals to other inputs in the production process. Hence the increasing returns to scale may continue to persist. In modern literature on economic growth, this aspect of transmission of the economic benefits of the expanding knowledge capital of the industry has been strongly emphasized as the prime mover of overall growth. Finally, an expansion of the industry output or knowledge capital may lead to a better trained and more efficient labor force with a consequent reduction in the costs of the j-th firm. Learning by doing and the rapid transmission of knowledge across industries and firms play a very dynamic impact in firm's growth.

Consider for example a nonlinear cost function $C_j = F_j(y_j, y_T)$ specifying the long run costs of firm j depending on the industry output $y_T = \sum_{j=1}^{n} y_j$ level as well as its own output level. Maximizing the profit function $\pi_j = py_j - C_j$ we obtain the condition price equaling marginal cost i.e., $p = MC_j = \partial F_j / \partial y_j$. Assuming that the second order condition $\partial^2 F_j / \partial y_j^2 > 0$ is satisfied we obtain the supply functions $S_j = y_j$ for n firms $S_j = S_j(p)$ with an aggregate supply $S = \sum_{j=1}^{n} S_j$. Each supplier bases his behavior on his own MC curve. Each anticipates the total industry output and selects his optimal output to equate price and marginal cost. If all suppliers anticipate the same industry output and if this industry output is consistent with their individual output levels, no further adjustment is needed: total demand equals total supply and the equilibrium price is the market clearing price. Otherwise some or all individual MC curves will shift from their anticipated levels and suppliers will adjust levels correspondingly. This is the Walrasian adjustment process under competition, which will continue till the market reaches its equilibrium, when no further adjustments are needed.

To consider an example we specify a cost-oriented DEA model as follows:

Min θ

s.t. $\sum_{j=1}^{n} C_j \lambda_j \leq \theta C_h ; \sum_{j=1}^{n} y_j \lambda_j \geq y_h$ (18)

$\sum_{j=1}^{n} y_j y_T \lambda_j = \phi_h y_T^2 ; \Sigma \lambda_j = 1 ; \lambda_j \geq 0$

Here ϕ_h is the share of firm h in total industry output y_T and the constraint $\sum_j y_j y_T \lambda_j = \phi_h y_T^2$ states that $\sum_j y_j \lambda_j = \phi_h y_T = \hat{y}_h$ where $\hat{y}_h = \phi_h y_T$ i.e., the size of firm h in terms of the total industry output equals the weighted average output. If firm j is efficient in terms of the LP model (18) with a given ϕ_h ($0 < \phi_h < 1$), then its cost frontier can be written as

$$\beta C_j = \beta_0 + \alpha y_j + a y_j y_T \tag{19}$$

or $\quad C_j = \gamma_0 + \gamma_1 y_j + \gamma_2 y_j y_T$

where $\gamma_0 = \beta_0/\beta, \gamma_1 = \alpha/\beta, \gamma_2 = a/\beta$. Here we have imposed the third constraint as equality, so that the parameter a can have any sign: positive, negative or zero. The industry now sets up the efficiency model

$$\text{Min} \sum_{j=1}^{n} C_j$$

$$\text{s.t.} \sum_{j=1}^{n} y_j \geq D, y_j \geq 0 \tag{20}$$

where p is the Lagrange multiplier for the demand constraint $y_T \geq D$, with a fixed level of D.

On solving this problem one obtains in equilibrium

$$p = MC_j = \gamma_{0j} + \gamma_{1j} y_T + \gamma_{2j} y_j \tag{21}$$

If all firms have identical cost frontiers so that $y_j = y_T/n$, then we obtain the Cournot-type solution as

$$y_T = \frac{n}{n\gamma_1 + \gamma_2} p - \frac{n\gamma_0}{n\gamma_1 + \gamma_2} = (p/\gamma_1) - \gamma_0 \quad \text{for } n \to \infty$$

$$y_j = \frac{p}{n\lambda_1 + \gamma_2} - \frac{\gamma_0}{n\gamma_1 + \gamma_2}$$

If the firms have different cost functions each satisfying the cost frontier condition (20), then we have to solve n equations in (21) simultaneously in order to obtain an equilibrium output y_j^* such that $\Sigma y_j^* = y_T^*$ and $S(p^*) = D(p^*)$.

Note that if a is negative in the cost frontier (19), then we have external economies of scale and a positive value denotes external diseconomies for the j-th firm. The sharing parameter ϕ_h shows that different types of cost frontiers would result for different values of ϕ_h i.e., equal sharing may not always be optimal.

To conclude this chapter one may mention two features characterizing the high-tech industries today, which are heavily dependent on the use of computers in the production and distribution phases. One is the sharing of information about the changes in the new technology. Pooling of such information by firms allows them to exploit the external economies at a more intensive level. Secondly, networking through pooling of R&D investments is increasingly adopted by modern firms with the intention of reducing average costs and prices. This is especially true in the computer industry, where miniaturization and division of skills have helped to reduce unit costs and prices of computers, where the trend is towards reducing price by more than 10% per year. Thus input sharing in the form of knowledge sharing is likely to play an active role in the computer industry for now and the future.

References

- Johansen, K. (1982): Aggressiveness in the Core. Journal of Economic Behavior and Organization 3, 1-14
- Lu, D. (2001): Shared Network Investment. Journal of Economics 73, 299-312
- Lucas, R.E. (1993): Making a Miracle. Econometrica 61, 251-272
- Sengupta, J.K. (2000): Dynamic and Stochastic Efficiency Analysis: Economics of Data Envelopment Analysis. World Scientific Publishers, London

8
Modeling and Data Problems

Data envelopment analysis provides a nonparametric method of analysis of economic efficiency, in the sense that it does not have to assume any specific form of the production and cost frontier. By using the observed input output data it provides by the convex hull method an estimate of the production and cost frontier. The LP model is generally employed to estimate the frontier, which yields a piecewise linear function. Recently DEA models have been applied to private sector firms and enterprises, where data on market prices of inputs and outputs are available. In such cases the allocative efficiency concept is more appropriate, where prices present an important role. Also the need for linearity in the cost and production frontiers is much less compelling. The need for exploring some transformations of the input output data e.g., log transformation is likely to be useful. For example in modern high-tech industries the effects of inputs such as R&D investment and new innovation are strongly nonlinear. Hence we need to extend the DEA models accordingly.

The information contained in the data set also requires an intensive scrutiny, particularly when it contains noise elements. For time series data we have the additional problems due to nonstationarity and heterogeneity. These problems tend to raise doubts about the structural meaning of the coefficients of the production and cost frontiers.

This chapter discusses a few points about modeling and data problems associated with the nonparametric and semiparametric models of efficiency measurement.

8.1 Modeling Issues

Two types of broad issues of modeling arise in connection with the formulation and application of DEA models. One is the transition from firm efficiency to industry efficiency. Different forms of market e.g., perfect, imperfect and oligopolistic competition are relevant at the industry level. Output prices determined in such markets influence the relative efficiency of firms in the industry. We have discussed in earlier chapters some forms of market structures but not all.

Secondly, when a subset of firms are judged to be inefficient by the DEA model the question arises whether the firms exit when their market share is greatly reduced, or they tend to learn and improve their efficiency by adjusting their inputs and output. Also there is a role for optimal regulation of inefficient firms. How to develop optimal regulatory rules for the relatively inefficient firms? Could we devise an optimal tax subsidy scheme? This question is most important for policy purposes.

The role of indivisibility of some inputs, which may generate substantial economies of scale, has not been incorporated in the standard DEA models. Yet its impact at the industry level may be substantial, particularly when firms pool their fixed indivisible inputs into a club or group. The transition from the short to the long run needs to be investigated here.

Finally, there is the case of market failure, when the firms' production process yields both private and public goods and the industry generates external economies and diseconomies for the individual firms. How one has to modify and generalize the DEA models to incorporate such situations? In monopolistic competition product differentiation through a variety of brands allows firms to set up barriers to competition through brand loyalty. Such situations make it difficult to define an industry comprising similar firms. Also jointness in cost for multi-product firms requires that we introduce nonlinearity in the production and cost functions of a DEA model.

8.2   DEA Models Under Nonstationarity

With time series data the inputs and outputs tend to change over time. Advances in technology tend to shift the production and cost frontiers. Hence technical efficiency needs to be estimated in a framework where there are strong time trends in inputs and output. The distinction between level efficiency and growth efficiency as discussed in earlier chapters comes into focus here. Growth efficiency essentially refers to the time shift of the production and cost frontiers, which may be largely due to technological change. In this section we discuss some methods of treating nonstationarity in the context of DEA models.

Data envelopment analysis is closely related to the method of least absolute value (LAV) estimation used to estimate a stochastic production frontier. Farrell (1957) noted this in his pioneering study, when he compared DEA production frontiers with average production functions estimated by the ordinary least squares (OLS) approach. Later Timmer (1971) and Sengupta (1990, 1996b) and others explicitly derived the linkages between DEA and other L_p-norm based estimates, where $p = 1$ is the LAV method, $p = 2$ is OLS and $p = \infty$ is the minimax estimate.

The DEA method of estimating technical efficiency by the convex hull procedure applies a series of linear programming (LP) models, one for each decision-making unit (DMU) or firm. This method of efficiency evaluation however is subject to three basic problems, when the input output data are generated by a stochastic mechanism. The first problem is that the observed statistical data at the boundaries of the convex hull of the production set play a more dominant role in estimation of the piece-wise production frontier and if these data close to the convex hull contain outliers or large errors, then the frontier estimates become unreliable. Second, the DEA method based as it is on the LAV method of statistical estimation has the additional restrictions imposed by the nonnegativity of error for each observation. Finally, if the input output data are nonstationary over time due to trends in mean or conditional variance the usual production frontier estimates by either corrected OLS or LAV method are not statistically valid, since the usual regression coefficients do not converge in probability as the sample size increases and by implication the DEA estimates share the same inconsistency. Usually the empirical DEA studies compute two groups of DMUs, one technically efficient and the other not efficient and then run OLS for the two groups to test if the difference in production frontiers is significantly different. The conventional statistics like Chow test or F and t tests are inapplicable in these cases due to nonstationarity of input output data.

Our objective in this section is two-fold. First, we consider the technical implications of simple types of nonstationarity, e.g., random walk model or, Arch (autoregressive conditional heteroscedasticity) in the context of DEA models and propose several types of transformations of the standard DEA model in order to handle nonstationarity. These transformations lead to semiparametric forms of DEA models. Second, we propose a method of smoothing technique such as exponential weighted forecasts (EWF) of the input output data. These smoothed data replace the observed data, where the smoothed data are used to compute DEA efficiency scores. These smoothed data may be viewed as temporally aggregated data, which may be updated every time new data become available. Since smoothed data are more filtered than the observed data, the DEA estimates or the COLS estimates are likely to be more robust.

Finally, the nonstationarity may sometimes arise due to trends in conditional variance of output as in Arch models in time series. In this case a two-stage transformation of the DEA model may be derived. We propose some transformations of the standard DEA model in input-oriented forms.

Random Walk Models

Consider for example one output y_t and one input x_t model of a production function, where each defines a random walk, i.e.,

$$y_t = y_{t-1} + u_t, u_t \text{ iid}(0,1)$$
$$x_t = x_{t-1} + v_t, v_t \text{ iid}(0,1) \tag{1}$$

Assume that x_t, y_t are uncorrelated nonstationary variables and hence if we run the regression

$$y_t = \beta_0 + \beta_1 x_t + \varepsilon_t; \varepsilon_t \text{ nonstationary} \tag{2}$$

it should generally be possible to accept the null hypothesis $H_0: \beta_1 = 0$, while the standard R^2 tends to zero. Hoever, because of the nonstationary nature of the data implying ε_t to be nonstationary also, both time series x_t and y_t are growting over time, hence the ordinary regression (2) picks up the correlation resulting in nonzero and significant estimate of β_1, though each series may be growing for different reasons. Thus a significant nonzero estimate of β_1 represents spurious regression and correlation. A similar result holds when x_t is a vector process, representing m inputs for example. As in linear regression the DEA model would also pick up spurious marginal coefficients like β_1, though they would not have any structural significance.

A second consequence of nonstationarity is that the short run effect may differ significantly from the long run or steady state effect. Since a firm observing its inefficiency in the short run would tend to improve in the long run and if it succeeds it would tend to be efficient in the long run, the dynamic adjustment process is very important. Consider for example, the linear model

$$y_t = \alpha_0 + \alpha_1 y_{t-1} + \gamma_0 x_t + \gamma_1 x_{t-1} + \varepsilon_t \tag{3}$$
$$\varepsilon_t \sim \text{white noise } (0, \sigma^2)$$

the short run effect of x_t on y_t is γ_0 but this is not the long run effect. The long run effect is given by $\beta_1 = (1 - \alpha_1)^{-1} (\gamma_0 + \gamma_1)$ assuming $|\alpha_1| < 1$ for convergence. This occurs when the model is in long run equilibrium, i.e.,

$$\overline{y} = \beta_0 + \beta_1 \overline{x}, \beta_0 = (1-\alpha_1)^{-1}\alpha_0$$

Clearly if y_t and x_t are in logarithmic units, then γ_0 is the short run input elasticity and β_1 is the long run elasticity and the latter is generally much higher than the short run elasticity. By separating the short run and long run components the linear model (3) can be written as an error correction model (ECM) as follows, as has been shown by Engle and Granger (1987):

$$\Delta y_t = \gamma_0 \Delta x_t - (1-\alpha_1)[y_{t-1} - \beta_0 - \beta_1 x_{t-1}] + \varepsilon_t \qquad (4)$$
$$\varepsilon_t \sim \text{white noise } (0,1)$$

Engle and Granger have shown that if both x_t and y_t are first difference stationary, i.e., $\Delta y_t = y_t - y_{t-1}$ and $\Delta x_t = x_t - x_{t-1}$ are stationary, then they may be cointegrated of order one, so that the ECM representation is unique and valid linear regressions or LAV estimations would apply. By implication the DEA model embodying this ECM formulation would have structural and not spurious relationships between the inputs and the output.

Three implications of the ECM formulation (4) are most important from an econometric viewpoint. First, if the x_t and y_t are both cointegrated of order one, so that their first differences are stationary, then standard regression results with t and F statistics are all valid and hence the transformed DEA model following the ECM (4) have structural significance, since the regressions are not spurious. Second, the short and long run production frontiers may be jointly specified in the ECM form. Thus if the long run equilibrium holds then we would have

$$y_{t-1} = \beta_0 + \beta_1 x_{t-1} \qquad (5)$$
i.e. $\quad \overline{y} = \beta_0 + \beta_1 \overline{x}$ at steady state

but in case of disequilibrium the steady state relation (5) fails to hold and then the full model (4) applies, where the firm tends to adjust over time, $(1-\alpha_1)$ being the speed of adjustment. The dynamic adjustment mechanism is then the cornerstone of the path of convergence to the long run or steady state equilibrium. Finally, the first order ECM model (4) can be more generalized to higher orders, e.g.,

$$A(L)\Delta y_t = B(L)\Delta x_t - (1-\alpha)[y_{t-p} - \beta_0 - \beta_1 x_{t-p}] + \varepsilon_t$$

where $A(L)$ and $B(L)$ are polynomials in the lag operator L. Clearly this type of ECM formulation could be developed for x_t being an m-element vector for each t, when (4) would represent a production frontier with m inputs yielding a single output.

Use of Transformations

We now consider a set of examples of transformation of standard DEA formulations, which can handle simple types of nonstationarity that arise in time series data on inputs and output. We consider one output and m inputs for simplicity and the extension to multi outputs is straightforward.

The first example is the case of a loglinear production function of DMU_j:

$$Y_j = \beta_0 + \sum_{i=1}^{m} \beta_i X_{ij} + \varepsilon_j \tag{6}$$

where $Y_j = \ln y_j$, $X_{ij} = \ln x_{ij}$, $\varepsilon_j = \ln e_j$. Here the error e is assumed to be lognormally distributed. Assume that Y_j and X_{ij} are each first difference stationary, i.e.,

$$\Delta Y_j = Y_j(t) - Y_j(t-1), \Delta X_{ij} = X_{ij}(t) - X_{ij}(t-1)$$

are stationary white noise processes. Then the appropriate input-oriented DEA model takes the form:

$$\text{Min } \theta_t$$
$$\text{s.t.} \sum_{j=1}^{N} (\Delta y_j / y_j(t))\lambda_{jt} \geq \Delta y_h / y_h(t)$$
$$\sum_{j=1}^{N} (\Delta x_{ij} / x_{ij}(t))\lambda_{jt} \leq \theta_t (\Delta x_{ih} / x_{ih}(t)) \tag{7}$$
$$\sum_{j=1}^{N} \lambda_{jt} = 1, \lambda_{jt} \geq 0; j = 1,...,N$$

If the optimal value θ_t^* of θ_t is 1.0 for t then DMU_h is *growth efficient*. If for a subset of $t \in \{1, 2, ..., T\}$, the condition $\theta_t^* = 1.0$ holds, then it is growth efficient over that subset.

This growth efficiency can be compared with *level efficiency*, when we replace $\Delta y_j/y_j(t)$ and $\Delta x_{ij}/x_{ij}(t)$ by the levels: $y_j(t)$ and $x_{ij}(t)$. Clearly the more the degree of nonstationarity, the more divergence of growth efficiency from level efficiency would result.

A second example uses an ECM model. For stationary input output data one can use one of the standard DEA models for each t as:

$$\text{Min } g_{ht} = \sum_{i=1}^{m} \beta_i x_{ih}(t)$$

$$\text{subject to } \quad \varepsilon_j(t) = \sum_{i=1}^{m} \beta_i x_{ij}(t) - y_j(t) \geq 0 \tag{8}$$

$$\beta_i \geq 0, i = 1, 2, \ldots, m$$

If however the inputs and output are each first difference stationary, then one can use a transformed ECM-type model for testing the technical efficiency of DMU_h as:

$$\text{Min } g_{ht} = \sum_{i=1}^{m} \gamma_i \Delta x_{ih}(t) + \theta \varepsilon_h(t-1)$$

$$\text{s.t. } \sum_i \gamma_i \Delta x_{ij}(t) + \theta \varepsilon_j(t-1) \geq \Delta y_j(t) \tag{9}$$

$$\varepsilon_j(t) = \sum_i \beta_i x_{ij}(t) - y_j(t)$$

$$\beta = (\beta_i) \geq 0, 0 < \theta < 1$$

Note that this model assumes for simplicity that the parameters $\beta = (\beta_i)$, $\gamma = (\gamma_i)$ and θ are all constants and each programming model tests the technical efficiency of DMU_h, so that by varying h one can trace out the piecewise efficiency frontier. Although this appears to be nonlinear in form, it can be solved by an LP routine by rewriting the constraints of (9) as

$$\sum_{i=1}^{m} \gamma_i \Delta x_{ij}(t) + \sum_i \delta_i x_{ij}(t-1) \geq \Delta y_j(t) + \theta y_j(t-1)$$

where $\delta_i = \theta \beta_i$. Once the parameters $\hat{\delta}_i$ and $\hat{\theta}$ are computed the parameters β_i can be obtained from $\hat{\beta}_i = \hat{\delta}_i / \hat{\theta}$.

This dynamic efficiency model has several interesting interpretations. Assume that the reference unit DMU_h is *dynamically efficient* in the sense that the following holds at t:

$$\sum_i \gamma_i^* \Delta x_{ih}(t) + \theta^*(\sum_i \beta_i^* x_{ih}(t-1) - y_h(t-1)) = \Delta y_h(t)$$

Then if θ^* is close to zero, one would have a production frontier with incremental inputs and output as

$$\Delta y_h(t) = \sum_{i=1}^{m} \gamma_i \Delta x_{ih}(t)$$

If one of the inputs is capital and its coefficient is γ_1^*, then γ_1^* would denote the incremental output-capital ratio. Secondly, if $\gamma^* = (\gamma_1^*)$ is a null vector and θ^* is positive, then the steady state production frontier is specified by

$$y_h(t-1) = \sum_{i=1}^{m} \beta_i^* x_{ih}(t-1)$$

which implies $\bar{y}_{h*} = \Sigma \beta_i^* \bar{x}_{ih}$ in the long run. Note that the intercept terms γ_0^* and β_0^* can also be easily introduced in this framework. Also, the parameter θ^* lying between zero and one may be interpreted as the correction factor or the utilization coefficient. Thus we have now three sources of dynamic efficiency: the level of past or lagged inputs, the incremental inputs and the degree of capacity utilization of the steady state input output relations. An empirical application by Sengupta (1992, 2000) of this type of model showed a striking difference between the two sets of input coefficients, namely γ_i^* and β_i^*.

Consider now a third example where the conditional variance of output is subject to a linear trend. A random walk model has this property. Let $y_j(t) = E_{t-1}(y_j(t)) + e_j(t)$ and $v_j(t) = E_{t-1}(e_j^2(t)), e_j(t) \sim NID(0, \sigma_j^2)$ be the conditional mean and variance of output $y_j(t)$, conditional on the information available up to time t-1. On using the empirical estimates $\hat{v}_j(t)$ the Arch (autoregressive conditional heteroscedastic) model tests the linear regression

$$\hat{v}_j(t) = a\hat{v}_j(t-1) + b\hat{v}_j(t-2) + \varepsilon_j(t); \varepsilon_j(t) \sim NID(0, \delta_\varepsilon^2) \tag{10}$$

on the conditional variances to find out if it shows persistent volatility. To incorporate this idea into the DEA model, we assume for simplicity that only the conditional output variances matter and the conditional input variances have no trend. Then we can represent one type of transformed DEA model as follows:

$$\text{Min } \theta_t$$
$$\text{s.t. } \sum_{j=1}^N \hat{x}_{ij}(t)\lambda_j(t) \leq \theta_t \hat{x}_{ih}(t)$$
$$\sum_{j=1}^N \hat{y}_j(t)\lambda_j(t) \geq \hat{y}_h(t)$$
$$\sum_{j=1}^N \hat{v}_j(t)\lambda_j(t) = \hat{v}_h(t)$$
$$\sum_{j=1}^N \hat{v}_j(t-1)\lambda_j(t) \leq \hat{v}_h(t-1) \tag{11}$$
$$\sum_{j=1}^N \hat{v}_j(t-2)\lambda_j(t) \leq \hat{v}_h(t-2)$$
$$\sum_{j=1}^N \lambda_j(t) = 1, \lambda_j(t) \geq 0$$

This model tests the relative efficiency of DMU$_h$ for each time point t, when the estimated conditional means of inputs and output and the estimated conditional variance of output enter into the dynamic production frontier. Note, that the third constraint is used here as an equality so that this dual variable is free in sign. Clerly if DMU$_h$ is efficient in the sense of $\theta_t^* = 1$ for some t or subinterval of the time domain, then it must hold

$$\hat{y}_j(t) = (\beta_0^*(t)/\alpha^*) + \Sigma \hat{x}_{ij}(t)(\beta_i^*/\alpha^*)$$
$$- (b_j^*/\alpha^*)v_j(t) + (c_j^*/\alpha^*)v_j(t-1) \tag{12}$$
$$+ (d_j^*/\alpha^*)v_j(t-2)$$

Clearly the conditional mean output on this efficiency frontier depends on its conditional variance and the conditional mean inputs. As in mean variance efficiency in portfolio theory, the conditional output variances represent output fluctuations on the average. As in CAPM (capital asset pricing model) of capital market efficiency, this formulation can directly test the riskiness of an efficient production function. When the conditional variances are dropped, we get back the standard production frontier.

Smoothing Techniques

Smoothing techniques refer to those statistical methods, which estimate the long run trends in input output data. The estimated data may then be used in estimating technical efficiency in the DEA model. These techniques are most useful in situations when model-based methods cannot be used. For example, available samples of data may be very small for LAV or other estimation methods. Also if the data have unit roots as in random walk, then smoothing techniques may produce optimal estimates of output and inputs, which may be used in DEA models.

Consider two examples. The first uses one-sided moving average of output and inputs as

$$\bar{y}_j(t) = (n+1)^{-1} \sum_{i=0}^{n} y_j(t-i)$$

$$\bar{x}_{ij}(t) = (n+1)^{-1} \sum_{i=0}^{n} x_{ij}(t-i) \qquad (13)$$

and then use these smoothed data $\bar{y}_j(t), \bar{x}_{ij}(t)$ in the transformed DEA model as follows:

$$\text{Min } \theta(t)$$
$$\text{s.t. } \sum_{j=1}^{N} \bar{x}_{ij}(t)\lambda_j(t) \leq \theta(t)\bar{x}_{ih}(t)$$
$$\sum_j \bar{y}_j(t)\lambda_j(t) \geq \bar{y}_h(t) \qquad (14)$$
$$\sum_j \lambda_j(t) = 1, \lambda_j(t) \geq 0$$

Let $\{\theta^*(t), \lambda_j^*(t); t = 1, 2, ..., T\}$ denote the efficiency based time series for the reference DMU$_h$ over time. The production frontier

$$\bar{y}_h(t) = (\beta_0^*/\alpha^*) + \sum_{i=1}^{m} (\beta_i^*/\alpha^*)\bar{x}_{ij}(t) \tag{15}$$

would then represent a long run production relation, which being based on smoothed data is likely to be more stable. However, an appropriate choice of n in (13) is needed for estimating the trend. A larger n means more smoothing, while a smaller n less smoothing.

We may also use this moving average procedure to *detrend* a series, e.g.,

$$\tilde{x}_{ij}(t) = x_{ij}(t) - \bar{x}_{ij}(t)$$
$$\tilde{y}_j(t) = y_j(t) - \bar{y}_j(t)$$

and then use these values of $\tilde{x}_{ij}(t)$ and $\tilde{y}_j(t)$ in the DEA model (14) instead of the observed values. This then identifies then short run production frontier for DMU$_h$ when it is efficient, i.e.,

$$\tilde{y}_h(t) = (\tilde{\beta}_0^*/\tilde{\alpha}^*) + \sum_{i=1}^{m} (\tilde{\beta}_i^*/\tilde{\alpha}^*)\tilde{x}_{ij}(t) \tag{16}$$

If the inputs and output are in logarithmic units, then the difference between the two sets of input elasticities $\{\bar{\gamma}_i^* = \beta_i^*/\alpha^*\}$ and $\{\tilde{\gamma}_i^* = \tilde{\beta}_i^*/\tilde{\alpha}^*\}$ may be analyzed to see if the short run impact is different from the long run. For example in some of the modern high-technology industries like computers and microelectronics, the impact of R&D expenditure on output productivity may differ significantly in the long run from the short run.

Now consider a second example where the exponentially weighted moving average method is used for smoothing. Each output $y_j(t)$ and input $x_{ij}(t)$ is now transformed as

$$\bar{y}_j(t) = \alpha y_j(t) + (1-\alpha)\bar{y}_j(t-1)$$
$$\bar{x}_{ij}(t) = \beta x_{ij}(t) + (1-\beta)\bar{x}_{ij}(t-1) \tag{17}$$

where the weights are in the domain $\{0 < \alpha < 1, 0 < \beta < 1\}$ for convergence. The optimal values of the weights α and β can be determined by following a method due to Muth (1960), which minimizes the variance, e.g., of $y_j(t)$ around $\bar{y}_j(t)$.

Two implications of this exponentially weighted smoothing (EWS) method are to be noted. First, one can rewrite (17) in an error correcting form with an updating sequence, e.g.,

$$\bar{y}_j(t) = \bar{y}_j(t-1) + \alpha(y_j(t) - \bar{y}_j(t-1))$$

where the error is $e(t) = y_j(t) - \bar{y}_j(t-1)$ and a fraction α of this error is used in updating the forecast value $\bar{y}_j(t)$.

Second, one could also write

$$\bar{y}_j(t) = \sum_{k=0}^{t-1} w_k y_j(t-k)$$

where $w_k = \alpha(1-\alpha)^k$. Thus if α is close to one, the recent observations get more weight so that in the limit $\alpha = 1.0$, past data have no influence on the smoothed data. If α is small, then the lagged or past values are important. Thus, if the fluctuations and noise in observed data are large, then a smaller value of α helps. The reverse holds for smaller fluctuations in observed data.

Kalman Filtering

Like EWS the method of Kalman filtering provides a recursive procedure of estimation in case of two kinds of errors, one in the system dynamics and the other as a measurement noise. By incorporating the time-varying variances for these errors, the estimates provide adaptivity to new information as it becomes available. Assume that for each DMU_j we have the input vector $x(t+1)$ and the output process $y(t)$ evolve as follows:

$$x(t+1) = x(t) + e(t+1)$$

$$y(t) = B\,x(t) + v(t)$$

where the errors e(t) and v(t) are assumed to be independent such that $E(e(t)e(t)') = R_1, E(v(t)v'(t)) = R_2$ and $E(v(t)) = 0, E(e(t)) = 0$ for all t.

The problem is to make an optimal prediction $\hat{x}(t+1)$ of x(t + 1) given the observations (y(t), y(t-1),...,y(0)) which have additive noise components. The prediction of x(t + 1) is now constructed by the linear decision rule

$$\hat{x}(t+1) = \hat{x}(t) + K(t)[y(t) - B\hat{x}(t)] \qquad (18)$$

where the Kalman gain matrix K(t) is to be optimally determined. Denote $(x(t) - \hat{x}(t))$ by $\tilde{x}(t)$ and then derive

$$\tilde{x}(t+1) = [I - K(t)B]\tilde{x}(t) + e(t+1) + K(t)v(t)$$

which has the mean $E\{\tilde{x}(t+1]\} = (I - K(t)B)E(\tilde{x}(t))$ which converges to zero if the initial value of $\tilde{x}(0)$ is fixed and the matrix [I-K(t) B] has all its eigenvalues less than unity in absolute value. Then it follows that the variance-covariance matrix V(t+1) of vector $\tilde{x}(t+1)$ satisfies the linear difference equation

$$V(t+1) = [I - K(t)B]V(t)(I - K(t)B)' + R_1 + K(t)R_2K'(t)$$

with the initial condition $V(0) = R_0$, where prime denotes the transpose. Now we choose the matrix K(t), also called Kalman gain matrix by a MSE (mean squared error) criterion, i.e., we choose K(t) so that it minimizes the variance of the scalar product $w'\tilde{x}(t+1)$, i.e., minimizes $w'V(t+1)$ w for nonzero weight vector w. The optimal value of K(t) denoted as K*(t) is then of the form:

$$K^*(t) = (IV(t)B') + R_1 - (IV(t)B')[R_2 + BV(t)B']^{-1}$$

when

$$V(t+1) = (IV(t)I') + R_1 - (IV(t)B')[R_2 + BV(t)B'][IV(t)I'] \qquad (19)$$

This equation (19) is called the Riccati equation which has to be recursively solved in order to provide an optimal update of the linear decision rule equation (18), i.e.,

$$\hat{x}(t+1) = \hat{x}(t) + K^*(t)[y(t) - B\hat{x}(t)]$$

One can then use these estimates $\hat{x}(t+1)$ and $\hat{y}(t) = B\hat{x}(t)$ in the transformed DEA model as

$$\text{Min } \theta(t+1)$$
$$\text{s.t.} \sum_{j=1}^{N} \hat{x}_j(t+1)\lambda_j(t+1) \leq \theta(t)\hat{x}_h(t+1)$$
$$\sum_{j=1}^{N} \hat{y}_j(t+1)\lambda_j(t+1) \geq \hat{y}_h(t+1)$$
$$\sum_j \lambda_j(t+1) = 1, \lambda_j(t+1) \geq 0, \text{ all } j$$

By moving t one step ahead we can generate optimal efficiency measures $\{\theta^*(t+1), t=1,2,\ldots,T\}$. Clearly these measures are likely to be more stable in the sense of optimal noise reduction. Note, the three features of the variance equation (19), which have to be recursively solved for computing the optimal Kalman gain matrices $K^*(t)$. The variance $V(t+1)$ is a matrix measure of the errors of prediction with three components: the first I V(t) I' shows how the error propagates to stage (t+1) through system dynamics, the second term R_1 shows the increase of error variances due to the disturbance e(t) and the third term shows how the measurement noise in output affects V(t+1) through the matrix R_2.

Control theory literature provides several efficient numerical algorithms for solving the Riccati equation (19) in variance and hence obtaining Kalman gain matrices $K^*(t)$. As in EWS the Kalman filtering technique is widely used in forecasting system dynamics from noisy input output data.

References

- Engle, R.F., Grange, C.W.J. (1987): Cointegration and Error Correction: Representation, Estimation and Testing. Econometrica 56, 251-276
- Muth, J.F. (1960): Optimal Properties of Exponentially Weighted Forecasts. Journal of American Statistical Association 55, 299-311
- Sengupta, J.K. (1990): Transformations in Stochastic DEA Models. Journal of Econometrics 46, 109-123
- Sengupta, J.K. (1992): Nonparametric Approach to Dynamic Efficiency: A Nonparametric Application of Cointegration to Production Functions. Applied Economics 24, 153-159

- Sengupta, J.K. (1996a): The Efficiency Distribution Approach in Data Envelopment Analysis: An Application. Journal of the Operational Research Society 47, 1387-1397
- Sengupta, J.K. (1996b): Recent Develpments in Data Envelopment Analysis: Theory and Applications. Applied Stochastic Models and Data Analysis 12, 1-26
- Sengupta, J.K. (2000): Dynamic and Stochastic Efficiency Analysis. World Scientific, Singapore
- Sengupta, J.K. (2002): Dynamic Production Frontier Analysis Under Uncertainty and Technical Change. Submitted for publication
- Timmer, C.P. (1971): Using a Probabilistic Frontier Production to Measure Technical Efficiency. Journal of Political Economy 79, 776-794

Index

access efficiency, 39
adjustment cost theory, 19
allocative efficiency, 93
asymmetric information, 5

capacity cost, 90
chance-constrained programming, 64
coalition, 148
COLS regression, 114
computer industry, 101
core, 147
cost efficiency models, 4
cost frontier, 6

data envelopment analysis, 10
DEA models under uncertainty, 7
decentralization aspects, 6
demand fluctuations, 62
dynamic cost frontier, 24
dynamic portfolio frontier, 134
dynamic production frontier, 24

ECM model, 165
economies of scope, 8
efficiency dynamics, 104
equilibrium, 93
EWF method, 163

game theory efficiency, 148
group efficiency, 152
growth efficiency, 38

HMMS model, 124
hypercompetition, 73

innovation efficiency, 70
input sharing, 147
IT investments, 11

Kalman filtering, 172
knowledge capital, 70

LAV method, 163
learning by doing, 16
learning curve effects, 108
limit pricing theory, 36
level efficiency, 71
L_p norm, 162

Malmquist index, 25
mean variance efficiency, 131
MES, 62

nonparametric estimation, 162
nonstationarity, 162

OLS method, 163

Pareto optimal, 70
principal-agent problem, 6
portfolio efficiency, 132
production frontier, 17

R&D inputs, 108
random walk, 163
rational expectations, 127
returns to scale, 102
robustness of solution, 130

scale efficiency, 112
semiparametric models, 15
shared investment, 152
Solow residual, 75
stationary series, 163
stochastic dominance, 137-140
stochastic efficiency, 11

technical efficiency, 9
technological progress, 34
TFP growth, 22, 41

Walrasian adjustment, 158
Walrasian tatonnement, 12

Druck: Strauss Offsetdruck, Mörlenbach
Verarbeitung: Schäffer, Grünstadt